ASBESTOS ESSENTIALS

TASK MANUAL

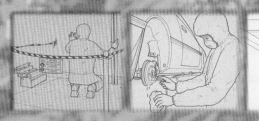

Task guidance sheets for the
building maintenance and allied trades

© *Crown copyright 2001*
Applications for reproduction should be made in writing to:
Copyright Unit, Her Majesty's Stationery Office,
St Clements House, 2-16 Colegate, Norwich NR3 1BQ

First published 2001

ISBN 0 7176 1887 0

This guidance is issued by the Health and Safety Executive.
Following the guidance is not compulsory and you are free to
take other action. But if you do follow the guidance you will
normally be doing enough to comply with the law. Health and
safety inspectors seek to secure compliance with the law and
may refer to this guidance as illustrating good practice.

CONTENTS

EQUIPMENT AND METHOD GUIDANCE SHEETS (EM) 1-8 (see overleaf)

TASK GUIDANCE SHEETS (A) 1-25 (see overleaf)

EQUIPMENT AND METHOD GUIDANCE SHEETS (EM)

TASK GUIDANCE SHEETS (A)

INTRODUCTION

What does this guidance tell you and who is it for?

This guidance tells you where you are most likely to find asbestos and how to protect yourself when working with it.

It will be particularly useful for anyone involved in building maintenance, repair or refurbishment work, such as plumbers, carpenters and electricians. It will also be useful to other workers, not normally associated with the building trade; for example computer installers, cabling installers, fire alarm installers and telecommunications engineers may also disturb asbestos during their work. Safety representatives will also find this guidance useful.

It contains a range of task guidance sheets and equipment and method guidance sheets which describe how the work should be carried out, what equipment to use and how to use it.

Comprehensive guidance for this type of work is given in *Introduction to asbestos essentials: Comprehensive guidance on working with asbestos in the building maintenance and allied trades* HSG213 HSE Books 2001 ISBN 0 7176 1901 X.

What is asbestos?

There are three main types of asbestos - chrysotile, amosite and crocidolite. They are usually called white, brown and blue asbestos respectively. However, they cannot be identified just by their colour. Laboratory analysis is required.

How does asbestos get into the body?

Asbestos fibres enter the body through the nose and mouth; they cannot be absorbed through your skin. The body naturally gets rid of any asbestos fibres that you might take in with food and water. The body will get rid of most of the larger fibres, but tiny fibres can pass into the lung where they can cause disease. They can stay there for many years.

It is because fibres can remain in the lungs for so long that small but repeated exposures on different jobs, over the years, can lead to the development of an asbestos-related disease. *This is why it is important to prevent or control exposure on every single job.*

Why is asbestos dangerous?

Breathing in asbestos fibres can lead to you developing one of three fatal diseases:

■ Asbestosis which is a scarring of the lung leading to shortness of breath.

■ Lung cancer.

■ Mesothelioma which is a cancer of the lining around the lungs and stomach.

There is no cure for asbestos-related diseases.

It is important to remember that people who smoke and are exposed to asbestos fibres are at even greater risk of developing lung cancer.

Asbestos-related diseases are currently responsible for about 3000 deaths a year in Great Britain. These diseases can take from 15 to 60 years to develop, from first exposure, so you would not be aware of any sudden change in your health after breathing in asbestos fibres.

Many of those suffering today from asbestos-related diseases worked in the building maintenance trades. They were carpenters, shopfitters, plumbers, electricians, gas service engineers etc. They were exposed to asbestos fibres in their day-to-day work with asbestos materials or because work with asbestos was carried out near them.

Where is asbestos found in buildings?

Asbestos materials have been put to many uses over the past century. A drawing of an 'asbestos building' is given on the inside cover. This shows you typical locations for the most commonly used asbestos materials. *However, it does not include all possible uses for asbestos materials which you may come across.*

The importation and use of blue and brown asbestos has been banned by law since 1985. In 1999 the importation, supply and use of white asbestos was also banned with the exception of a few specialised uses where there is no suitable substitute available. These will have ceased by 2005. But, many thousands of tonnes of asbestos were used in buildings in the past. Much of this is still there and you cannot easily identify it from its appearance.

Its most common uses were:

■ loose asbestos packing between floors and in partition walls;

■ sprayed ('limpet') asbestos on structural beams and girders;

■ lagging on pipework and boilers, calorifiers, heat exchangers etc;

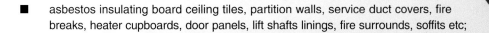

- asbestos insulating board ceiling tiles, partition walls, service duct covers, fire breaks, heater cupboards, door panels, lift shafts linings, fire surrounds, soffits etc;

- asbestos cement products such as roof and wall cladding, bath panels, boiler and incinerator flues, fire surrounds, gutters, rainwater pipes, water tanks etc; and

- other products such as floor tiles, mastics, sealants, decorative coatings, rope seals and gaskets (in pipework etc), millboard, paper products, cloth (fire blankets, etc) and bituminous products (roofing felt, etc).

See diagram of an 'asbestos building' (inside front cover)

How do I know if I am at risk?

If you come across any hidden or dusty materials which you suspect may contain asbestos, stop work and get advice. The person in charge of the job must find out if there is any asbestos on the site or assume that anything that looks like asbestos is asbestos. Identification of asbestos materials is not easy and you can only be sure if it has been tested by a specialist laboratory.

The risk of being exposed to asbestos is greatest when:

- you are working on an unfamiliar site;

- asbestos materials were not identified before the job started;

- asbestos materials were identified but the information was not given to the people doing the work;

- you do not know how to recognise and work safely with asbestos; and

- you know how to work safely but you *do not* use the proper precautions.

Remember, provided the asbestos material is in good condition and in a position where it cannot be easily damaged, it will not pose a risk to health.

What should those in charge of the job do?

They must:

- find out whether asbestos materials are present;

- where possible, plan the work to avoid disturbing the asbestos material;

- ensure that anyone who is going to work on asbestos materials is properly trained and supervised;

- decide whether or not the work needs to be carried out by a specialist contractor licensed by HSE, (see Figure 1, page 5);

■ assess the risk to your health from any work with asbestos and take the necessary precautions to do the job safely;

■ when dealing with asbestos remember other hazards, eg dealing with heights;

■ prevent or reduce asbestos exposure to the lowest level possible using the work procedures and control measures in these task guidance sheets and the equipment and method guidance sheets;

■ prepare a plan of work explaining what the job involves and the work procedures and control measures you need to use;

■ provide you with the right equipment which is clean and in good working order and gives protection against asbestos and train you in its proper use;

■ make sure the work area is visually inspected when the work is finished to make sure that it is fit for reoccupation;

■ decide if clearance testing is needed, the task guidance sheets tell you when it is necessary;

■ make arrangements for the safe disposal of any asbestos waste; and

■ consult the health and safety representative, if there is one, about the control measures.

What the law requires

Work with asbestos materials is covered by several sets of regulations, including:

■ *The control of asbestos at work. Control of Asbestos at Work Regulations 1987. Approved Code of Practice* L27 HSE Books 1999 ISBN 0 7176 1673 8

■ *A Guide to the Asbestos (Licensing) Regulations 1983: Guidance on Regulations* L11 HSE Books 1999 ISBN 0 7176 2435 8

■ *Asbestos (Prohibitions) Regulations 1992* SI1992/3067 The Stationery Office ISBN 0 1102 5740 5

■ *Managing construction for health and safety. Construction (Design and Management) Regulations 1994. Approved Code of Practice* L54 HSE Books 1995 ISBN 0 7176 0792 5 and *A guide to the Construction (Health, Safety and Welfare) Regulations 1996* INDG220 HSE Books 1996 ISBN 0 7176 1161 2

This guide covers work outside the Asbestos (Licensing) Regulations. The Asbestos (Licensing) Regulations require that work with asbestos insulation, asbestos coatings and asbestos insulating board must normally be carried out by a specialist contractor licensed by HSE. There are exceptions (see Figure 1, page 5).

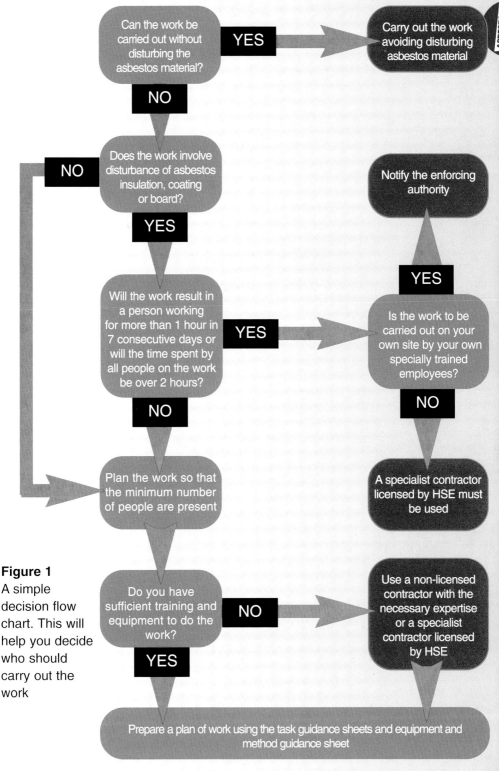

Can the work be carried out without disturbing the asbestos material?

YES → Carry out the work avoiding disturbing asbestos material

NO ↓

Does the work involve disturbance of asbestos insulation, coating or board?

NO →

YES ↓

Will the work result in a person working for more than 1 hour in 7 consecutive days or will the time spent by all people on the work be over 2 hours?

YES → Is the work to be carried out on your own site by your own specially trained employees?

YES → Notify the enforcing authority

NO → A specialist contractor licensed by HSE must be used

NO ↓

Plan the work so that the minimum number of people are present

Do you have sufficient training and equipment to do the work?

NO → Use a non-licensed contractor with the necessary expertise or a specialist contractor licensed by HSE

YES ↓

Prepare a plan of work using the task guidance sheets and equipment and method guidance sheet

Figure 1
A simple decision flow chart. This will help you decide who should carry out the work

REMEMBER: Any work that is outside the licensing regulations is still covered by CAW. The above flow chart (Figure 1) will help you decide if a specialist contractor licensed by HSE must carry out the work.

What can I do to protect myself?

Do:

- follow the plan of work, the task guidance sheets and equipment and method guidance sheets;

- make sure that you use the right sheet for the task;

- stop work if you find any material you suspect may contain asbestos;

- use the personal protective equipment given to you, including a respirator (mask);

- clean up as you go - don't let waste pile up;

- wash before you take a break; and at the end of the day's work (follow the procedure in the task guidance sheet);

- put asbestos waste in a suitable sealed container. You can use a heavy duty polythene bag, put it in a second bag, and label (Figure 2) the outer bag to show that it contains asbestos (remember: asbestos waste needs to be taken to a licensed tip).

Don't:

- use work methods which create a lot of dust;

- take home overalls you have worn while working with asbestos;

- eat or drink in the work area; or

- smoke.

Waste disposal

Figure 3 outlines how asbestos waste should be dealt with.

Further information on waste disposal can be obtained from the Environment Agency (Enquiry Line: 0645 333111) in England and Wales and the Scottish Environment Protection Agency in Scotland (Head Office: 01786 457700).

If you require detailed information on the carriage of asbestos by road or rail see the HSE leaflet: *Are you involved in the carriage of dangerous goods by road and rail?* INDG234(rev) HSE Books.

Figure 2: Labelling requirements for plastic bags/sacks containing asbestos waste

Proper shipping name	Class number	
Waste blue asbestos (crocidolite)	UN 2212	Carriage of Dangerous Goods (Classification, Packaging and
Waste brown asbestos (amosite)	UN 2212	Labelling) and Use of Transportable Pressure
Waste white asbestos (chrysotile)	UN 2590	Receptacles Regulations 1996 Regulations 7 and 8 refer

Danger sign

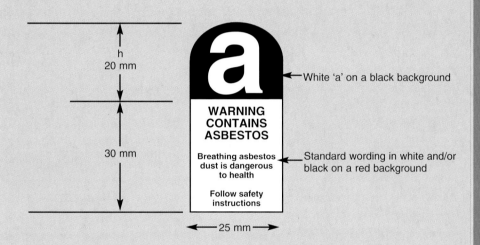

The dimensions in millilitres of the label shall be those shown on the diagram, except that larger measurements may be used, but in that case the dimension of the label indicated as h, on the diagram above, shall be 40% of the dimension indicated as H on that diagram.

The label shall be clearly and indelibly printed so that the words in the lower half of the label can be easily read, and those words shall be printed in black or white.

Figure 3: Procedure for dealing with asbestos waste

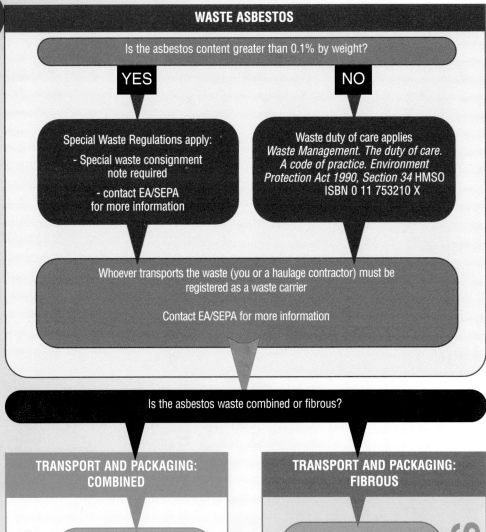

WASTE ASBESTOS

Is the asbestos content greater than 0.1% by weight?

YES / NO

Special Waste Regulations apply:
- Special waste consignment note required
- contact EA/SEPA for more information

Waste duty of care applies
Waste Management. The duty of care. A code of practice. Environment Protection Act 1990, Section 34 HMSO ISBN 0 11 753210 X

Whoever transports the waste (you or a haulage contractor) must be registered as a waste carrier

Contact EA/SEPA for more information

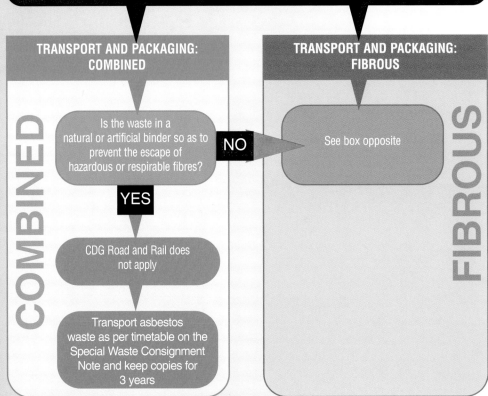

Is the asbestos waste combined or fibrous?

TRANSPORT AND PACKAGING: COMBINED

TRANSPORT AND PACKAGING: FIBROUS

COMBINED

Is the waste in a natural or artificial binder so as to prevent the escape of hazardous or respirable fibres?

NO → See box opposite

YES

CDG Road and Rail does not apply

Transport asbestos waste as per timetable on the Special Waste Consignment Note and keep copies for 3 years

FIBROUS

FIBROUS

Introduction

The waste is dangerous for transport, CDG Road and Rail applies

Asbestos cannot be transported in bulk, it must be packed in UN approved packages displaying:

- Proper shipping name
- Class number
- Danger sign (see Figure 2)

Does the vehicle in which the waste is to be transported have a maximum weight in excess of 3.5 tons?

YES

- Driver to be trained for Class 9 Dangerous Goods

- Vehicle to be fitted with a 2 kg dry powder extinguisher in cab (>3.5 tonnes - 6 kg)

- Emergency information (Tremcard) to be provided to the driver

NO

Does the weight of the asbestos exceed:
- Blue or brown - 200g?
- White - 500g?

YES

Are the packages of asbestos to be carried in a vehicle or in a bulk container on a vehicle?

NO

Bulk container | **Vehicle**

Transport as per timetable on the Special Waste Consignment Note

- Vehicle to display **orange panel** at front and rear
- Danger signs to be displayed on at least one side of the bulk container

Vehicle to display **orange panel** at front and rear

Special Waste Consignment Note to be kept by the consignor for three years. Other documentation to be kept by the operator for three months.

Key

EA: Environment Agency

SEPA: Scottish Environment Protection Agency

CDG Road and Rail: five sets of regulations (see 'Waste disposal' page 6)

Task guidance sheets and equipment and method guidance sheets

The task guidance sheets give practical guidance on how 25 common tasks can be safely carried out. It is important that a task guidance sheet is only used for the task it is meant for.

The task guidance sheets refer to a range of equipment and methods which must be followed so as to make sure that the guidance is effective. The equipment and method guidance sheets describe the equipment and how to use it. The task guidance sheets tell you when to consult a particular equipment and method guidance sheet.

DON'T FORGET

Be alert at all times to the dangers of working with old materials that may contain asbestos. If you come across asbestos - stop work and tell your supervisor. Avoid exposure to all dust. Follow the advice in this manual and protect your health and that of your workmates. Encourage them to do the same.

Further information

Access to further advice can be obtained from the British Institute of Occupational Hygienists (BIOH - 01332 298087), Asbestos Testing and Consultancy (ATAC) which is a division of ARCA (Asbestos Removal Contractors Association - 01283 531126), Asbestos Control and Abatement Division (ACAD) - 01325 466704, your trade association or the HSE InfoLine (08701 545500).

You are strongly advised to also consult the main guidance: *Introduction to asbestos essentials: Comprehensive guidance on working with asbestos in the building maintenance and allied trades* HSG213 HSE Books 2001 ISBN 0 7176 1901 X.

You can also find out more about working with asbestos from your safety representative, the nearest office of the Health and Safety Executive, or your Local Authority Environmental Health Department, which is listed in your telephone directory.

Further information on training can be found in the Approved Code of Practice *The Control of Asbestos at Work: Control of Asbestos at Work Regulations 1987: Approved Code of Practice* L27 HSE Books 1999 ISBN 0 7176 1673 8.
Details on organisations providing training can be obtained from HSE's InfoLine (08701 545500).

Free leaflets include:

Asbestos alert for building maintenance, repair and refurbishment workers INDG188P HSE Books 1995 Pocket card.

Working with asbestos in buildings INDG289 HSE Books 1999 (Also available in packs of 10 with ISBN 0 7176 1697 5).

HSE priced and free publications are available by mail order from HSE Books, PO Box 1999, Sudbury, Suffolk CO10 6FS. Tel: 01787 881165 Fax: 01787 313995. Website: www.hsebooks.co.uk (HSE priced publications are also available from bookshops).

For information about health and safety ring HSE's InfoLine Tel: 08701 545500, Fax: 02920 859260, e-mail: hseinformationservices@natbrit.com or write to HSE Information Services, Caerphilly Business Park Caerphilly CF83 3GG. You can also visit HSE's Website: www.hse.gov.uk.

While every effort has been made to ensure the accuracy of the references listed in this publication, their future availability cannot be guaranteed.

ASBESTOS GUIDANCE

What to do if you uncover asbestos materials or they are damaged during the task

Description

During the task you may come across asbestos materials which had not been found before you started. Also, when working on asbestos materials they may be accidentally damaged.

In either case it is important that you know what to do to:

● decide who must do the work;

● minimise the spread of contamination to nearby areas;

● keep exposure as low as reasonably practicable; and

● clean up the contamination.

Figure 4 outlines the actions you can take in these circumstances.

Check it out before you start work

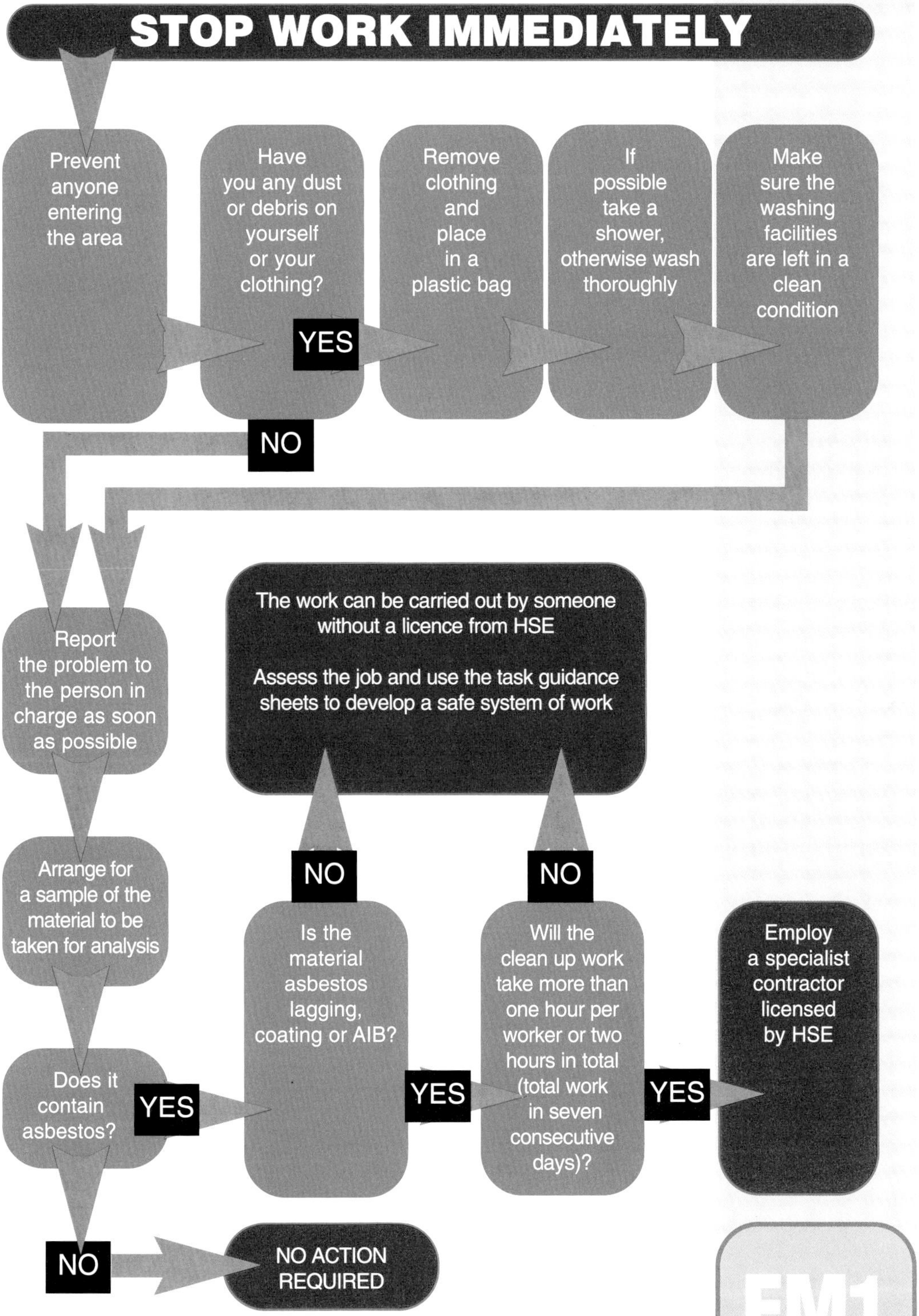

STOP WORK IMMEDIATELY

Prevent anyone entering the area	Have you any dust or debris on yourself or your clothing?	Remove clothing and place in a plastic bag	If possible take a shower, otherwise wash thoroughly	Make sure the washing facilities are left in a clean condition

YES

NO

Report the problem to the person in charge as soon as possible

The work can be carried out by someone without a licence from HSE

Assess the job and use the task guidance sheets to develop a safe system of work

Arrange for a sample of the material to be taken for analysis

NO

Is the material asbestos lagging, coating or AIB?

NO

Will the clean up work take more than one hour per worker or two hours in total (total work in seven consecutive days)?

Employ a specialist contractor licensed by HSE

Does it contain asbestos?

YES

YES

YES

NO

NO ACTION REQUIRED

Figure 4 One course of action you can take if you realise that you may be working on asbestos materials that you had not been warned about, or they are accidently damaged during the job

EM1
EQUIPMENT AND METHOD GUIDANCE SHEET

REMEMBER TO READ THE SAFETY CHECKLIST

ASBESTOS GUIDANCE

Training

Description

It is important that people carrying out *any* work on asbestos materials are properly trained and supervised.

If you do not have the right training and/or the job is not adequately supervised there is a strong possibility that the work will not be carried out properly. This can result in you and others being exposed to asbestos fibres.

HSE video: How are you today? The risks of asbestos in buildings Video cassette HSE Books 2001 ISBN 0 7176 1945 1

You need this training even if you have worked with asbestos in the past. You may have forgotten parts of any training you received; the training may not have been adequate; there may be new work methods available.

If you are self-employed you will need to obtain this training yourself (see Further information, page 11). If you are an employee, your employer should arrange for you to be trained.

Training

This is a requirement of regulation 7 of the Control of Asbestos at Work Regulations (CAW) *The control of asbestos at work.Control of Asbestos at Work Regulations 1987. Approved Code of Practice* L27 HSE Books 1999 ISBN 0 7176 1673 8 and should include, in the necessary detail, the following topics:

■ The effects asbestos can have on your health, including the added danger of smoking.

■ The presence of other hazards such as work at heights etc.

■ The uses and locations of asbestos materials in buildings and plant.

■ The type of work you are allowed to do by law.

■ What the CAW Regulations require you to do.

■ Work methods and equipment you need to use to do the task properly.

■ The correct choice, use and maintenance of personal protective equipment.

■ Decontamination procedures.

REMEMBER TO READ THE SAFETY CHECKLIST

- Maintenance of control measures.

- Emergency procedures.

- Waste disposal.

Trainees

If you are a young worker or a trainee it is important that particular attention is paid to your training. You may be at special risk because of your lack of experience.

Refresher training

This is required every year or more often where:

- Work methods change.

- The type of equipment changes.

- The type of work changes significantly.

Information and training of others

- People who may be affected by your work need to be given information and training.

- This should cover possible risks such as rearranged fire exits, as well as risks from the work on asbestos.

Supervision

The task should be supervised to make sure it is carried out properly.

Future developments

HSE is developing asbestos awareness material for use in the existing National Vocational Qualification/Scottish Vocational Qualification courses, for construction and related industries. This material is supported by a video which shows the risks of unknowingly disturbing asbestos materials. Also HSE and the National Training Organisations of the Construction Forum have jointly produced basic asbestos awareness pocket cards/leaflets which will be distributed to employers and workers in those industries. The training material, video and the pocket cards will be available from HSE Books/HSE Videos.

Further information

- *The control of asbestos at work. Control of Asbestos at Work Regulations 1987. Approved Code of Practice* L27 HSE Books 1999 ISBN 0 7176 1673 8

- Further information on organisations providing training can be obtained from HSE's InfoLine (08701 545500)

EM2

EQUIPMENT AND METHOD GUIDANCE SHEET

REMEMBER TO READ THE SAFETY CHECKLIST

EM3
EQUIPMENT AND METHOD GUIDANCE SHEET

Building a 'mini-enclosure' for the removal of a single asbestos insulating board ceiling tile

Equipment

- Proprietary 'mini-enclosures' are available (see further information). Alternatively you can construct your own.

- 1000 gauge polythene sheeting and duct and masking tape.

- Timber or other materials to build a frame.

- Smoke tubes.

- Garden type spray.

- Sealant, eg polyvinyl acetate (PVA).

- Suitable asbestos waste container, eg a labelled polythene sack.

Description

This guidance sheet explains how to build a 'mini-enclosure' to prevent the spread of asbestos during the removal of a single ceiling tile more than 0.36 m² in area eg 60 cms x 60 cms (see A2 'Removal of a single asbestos insulating board ceiling tile').

This sheet is not appropriate for the building of full enclosures for work which MUST be carried out by a specialist contractor licensed by HSE.

Use

A 'mini-enclosure' is used to prevent the spread of asbestos. A 'mini-enclosure' will not prevent or control exposure to asbestos fibres during the task, you do this by using the method in the task guidance sheet.

> **REMEMBER - You must include the time needed to build and dismantle the enclosure when deciding if you can do the work (see Figure 1, page 5).**

Building the enclosure

This work may be carried out at height. If so, the appropriate precautions MUST be taken to prevent falls (see *Tower scaffolds* Construction Information Sheet CIS10 HSE Books 1997 and *General access scaffolds and ladders* Construction Information Sheet CIS49 HSE Books 1997).

- Restrict access, eg close the door and/or use warning tape and notices.

- Erect access platform as necessary.

- The enclosure should be big enough to allow the work to be carried out safely.

- Where possible use a proprietary 'mini-enclosure'. These are quicker and easier to erect.

- Alternatively use timber or other materials to build a frame.

- Use duct tape to attach the polythene sheeting to the inner surface of the frame - this minimises cleaning.

REMEMBER TO READ THE SAFETY CHECKLIST

- Use masking tape to seal to the ceiling – do not use spray adhesive.

- Care needs to be taken if you seal to adjacent ceiling tiles - if the seal is too strong it will damage the material during dismantling.

- Make a slit in one wall to permit entry/exit. Reinforce with duct tape.

- Cover the entry/exit point with polythene sheeting. Attach to the enclosure by the top of the sheet.

- Use smoke tubes to check for leaking seals on either proprietary or constructed 'mini-enclosures' (See Figure 5).

- Release smoke at seals inside the enclosure. A second person can check for leaks outside.

- Seal leaks.

- Place tools, waste containers; bucket of water and rags etc in the enclosure (Figure 6).

Figure 5   Testing seal with a smoke tube, with second person using a torch to check for smoke leaking from seals

Dismantling the enclosure

Careful dismantling is very important.

- Using the Type H vacuum cleaner, clean the enclosed area.

- Use wet rags to clean the equipment.

- Use wet rags to clean the polythene sheeting.

- Visually inspect the enclosure to make sure that it has been properly cleaned.

- Spray the polythene sheeting with PVA.

- Carefully remove the polythene sheeting from the framework and place in the waste container.

- The framework can be re-used as long as it had been protected and is clean.

Further information

Information on the suppliers of proprietary enclosure framework can be obtained from the Asbestos Removal Contractors Association (ARCA): 01283 531126; ACAD (Asbestos Control and Abatement Division): 01325 466704 or the HSE InfoLine (08701 545500)

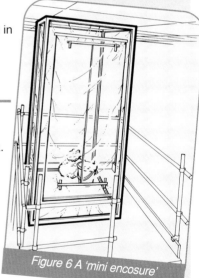

Figure 6 A 'mini encosure'

EM3

EQUIPMENT AND METHOD GUIDANCE SHEET

REMEMBER TO READ THE SAFETY CHECKLIST

ASBESTOS GUIDANCE

Using a Type H vacuum cleaner when working with asbestos

Description

This guidance sheet explains what a Type H vacuum cleaner is; how to use it to minimise the release of asbestos fibres during a task and how to use it to clean contaminated items.

Type H vacuum cleaners

Type H vacuum cleaners are designed to a British Standard (BS5415) (see *Safety of electrical motor-operated industrial and commercial cleaning appliances. Particular requirements. Specification for vacuum cleaners, wet and/or dry. Specification for type H industrial vacuum cleaners for dusts hazardous to health* BS 5415 2.2 Supplement No 1: 1986) and are the only type which should be used with asbestos (Figure 7).

They have special filters (HEPA - High Efficiency Particle Arrestor) which remove asbestos fibres from the air being blown out.

Most domestic type vacuums cleaners do not have HEPA filters and would blow fibres back to the atmosphere. These and domestic type vacuum cleaners with HEPA filters, but not to BS5415, should not be used.

- Type H vacuum cleaners come with a range of attachments.

- Type H vacuum cleaners can be purchased or hired.

- Make sure hired units are clean and in good working condition on receipt.

Vacuuming

- Pick up bigger pieces of debris and place in a suitable waste container.

- Carry out cleaning with care otherwise asbestos fibres can be disturbed and made airborne where they can be breathed in.

- Vacuuming very wet material can damage the HEPA filter.

- Use an adjustable floor attachment to clean floors, carpets and fabrics.

- Use a long, tapered attachment to clean areas with limited access.

- Use a flat attachment to clean solid surfaces such as desk tops as brush attachments can be difficult to clean.

*Figure 7
Schematic diagram
of a Type H vacuum
cleaner*

REMEMBER TO READ THE SAFETY CHECKLIST

Use as a control measure

- You can use a Type H vacuum cleaner to control exposure to asbestos fibres.

- Shadow vacuuming: Hold the nozzle as close as possible to the task eg removing a screw (Figure 8).

- Local extraction: The tool, eg drill bit, is enclosed (Figure 9).

- The nozzle of a Type H vacuum cleaner is attached to the plastic 'enclosure' where it draws away the dust.

Figure 8 Shadow vacuuming

Emptying and cleaning Type H vacuum cleaners

Emptying and cleaning Type H vacuum cleaners without the proper precautions will result in you, and other people, being exposed to high levels of asbestos fibres.

Figure 9 Using a plastic 'enclosure' when drilling a hole

- Do not empty or clean the inside of the Type H vacuum cleaner yourself - get this done by someone with the proper facilities, eg a specialist contractor licensed by HSE.

- Use the Type H vacuum cleaner and wet rags to clean the outer casing and attachments after each task.

- Visually inspect the casing, hose and attachments to make sure they have been cleaned properly.

- Keep the hose and attachments in a labelled plastic sack.

- When not in use place the sealing cap over the hose opening in the casing.

Problems

- Use of a long extension cable can result in low supply voltage and reduced suction.

- Reduced suction may mean the waste bag needs emptying.

- Reduced suction may mean the hose is blocked. Clear with care otherwise asbestos may be forcibly blown from the hose.

Further information

Information on the suppliers of plastic 'enclosures' can be obtained from the Asbestos Removal Contractors Association (ARCA): 01283 531126; ACAD (Asbestos Control and Abatement Division): 01325 466704 or the HSE InfoLine (08701 545500)

EM4
EQUIPMENT AND METHOD GUIDANCE SHEET

REMEMBER TO READ THE SAFETY CHECKLIST

ASBESTOS GUIDANCE

Wetting asbestos materials

Equipment

- Wetting agent. This can be obtained from a number of suppliers (see Further information).

- Liquid detergent can be used as an alternative.

- Sprayer, either a garden type spray or low pressure spraying machine (less than 3.4 bar (50 psi)) - this will prevent unnecessary disturbance of the fibres during application.

Description

This guidance sheet explains why you should wet asbestos materials before working on them and how this can be done.

It is important that you make sure that the asbestos material is wet. Otherwise you can be exposed to high concentrations of asbestos fibres.

The spraying technique can be used when painting asbestos materials.

Some tasks will be carried out at heights, if so, you MUST make sure that wetting does not present a risk of slips.

Use

- Wetting asbestos materials will reduce the number of asbestos fibres released during the work.

- Working on dry asbestos materials will result in high exposures to asbestos fibres.

- Wetting agents make it easier to wet asbestos fibres - blue and brown asbestos do not readily absorb water.

- Some asbestos materials, for example boards and sheets, cannot be easily wet all the way through, so you will also need to use other methods such as a Type H vacuum cleaner (see EM4 - Using a Type H vacuum cleaner when working with asbestos) to further control exposure.

- Note - vacuuming very wet material can damage the HEPA filter on the Type H vacuum cleaner.

Problems with using wetting agents

- Wetting agents may cause skin problems - consult manufacturers' material safety data sheet.

- Do not use if electrical equipment cannot be isolated or protected.

- Avoid use if there is potential for contact with chemicals which may present toxic or fire risks.

REMEMBER TO READ THE SAFETY CHECKLIST

- In these cases, other measures should be used to prevent asbestos fibres becoming airborne, for example, shadow vacuuming (see EM4 - Using a Type H vacuum cleaner when working with asbestos).

Procedure

- Dilute wetting agent according to the manufacturers' recommendations, usually between 10:1 and 15:1. Alternatively, dilute liquid detergent 8:1 with water.

- For the purposes of this guidance, spraying is the preferred method for wetting asbestos materials.

- Do not over wet.

- Carry out spraying carefully to avoid disturbing the asbestos or leaving dry patches (Figure 10).

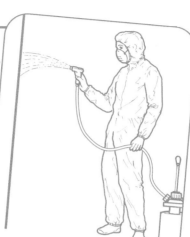

Figure 10 Spraying asbestos insulating board

- Spray using a slow backward and forward motion, avoiding concentrating on any one area as this can result in disturbance of the asbestos material.

- Allow the spray to 'fall' onto the asbestos material.

Further information

Information on the suppliers of wetting agents can be obtained from the Asbestos Removal Contractors Association (ARCA): 01283 531126; Asbestos Control and Abatement Division (ACAD): 01325 466704 or the HSE InfoLine (08701 545500)

EM5
EQUIPMENT AND METHOD
GUIDANCE SHEET

REMEMBER TO READ THE SAFETY CHECKLIST

ASBESTOS GUIDANCE

Personal protective equipment

Description

This guidance sheet describes the type of personal protective equipment (PPE) you will need to wear when carrying out the tasks covered by the Task Guidance Sheets.

PPE is the last line of defence. It is important that you follow the methods described in the task guidance sheets so that you minimise the amount of fibres which get into the air.

Footwear

■ Boots are preferable to disposable overshoes - these can present a risk of slips.

■ Do not use laced boots - laced boots can be difficult to clean.

Overalls

■ Disposable overalls are preferable to cotton - they do not need to be laundered.

■ Waterproof overalls may be required when working outdoors.

■ Wear one size too big - this will prevent ripping at the seams.

■ If the cuffs are loose, seal with tape.

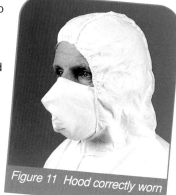

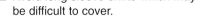
Figure 11 Hood correctly worn

■ Avoid long sleeve shirts which may be difficult to cover.

■ Wear legs over footwear - do not tuck into boots as dust can get in the top.

■ Wear the hood over the straps of the respirator (Figure 11).

■ Do not take used overalls home.

■ Dispose of used overalls in a suitable asbestos waste container.

REMEMBER TO READ THE SAFETY CHECKLIST

Respiratory protective equipment (RPE)

The task guidance sheets recommend the type of RPE to be worn. Make sure the assessment of the job confirms the type of respirator.

For the purposes of this guidance a disposable particulate respirator (FF P3) will normally be adequate.

- You need to be clean shaven.

- The respirator should be suitable for work with asbestos (Figure 12).

- The respirator should fit the wearer and be suitable for the task (Figure 13).

- Make sure you have been fit tested to the type of respirator you have chosen - consult your supplier.

- Make sure the respirator is worn correctly (Figures 13 and 14).

- Place straps firmly around the top and back of your head.

- The face piece should be tight to your face.

- Pinch the top of the respirator over your nose.

- Put the hood of your overalls over the straps.

- Put spectacles on after the respirator - otherwise they will create a gap between the RPE and face.

- Do not leave the respirator lying around where it can collect dust.

- Do not wear the respirator around your neck or on your head when not in use.

- At the end of the shift dispose of used RPE in a suitable asbestos waste container.

Figure 12 The wrong type of respirator (One for use with general dust, doubled up to 'try' and give more protection)

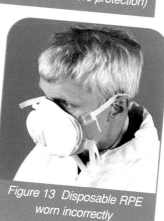

Figure 13 Disposable RPE worn incorrectly

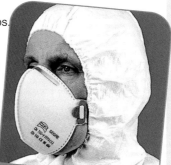

Figure 14 Disposable RPE worn correctly

Information on the suppliers of protective equipment can be obtained from the Asbestos Removal Contractors Association (ARCA): 01283 531126; Asbestos Control and Abatement Division (ACAD): 01325 466704 or the HSE InfoLine (08701 545500)

EM6

EQUIPMENT AND METHOD GUIDANCE SHEET

REMEMBER TO READ THE SAFETY CHECKLIST

ASBESTOS GUIDANCE

EM7

EQUIPMENT AND METHOD
GUIDANCE SHEET

Using rags to clean surfaces and equipment contaminated with asbestos

Description

This guidance sheet explains how to use rags to wipe clean minor asbestos contamination on smooth surfaces and equipment used for work on asbestos materials.

Materials

- Either cotton rags (which do not leave bits of fabric on clean surfaces) or impregnated rags (eg 'Tak' rags).

- Adhesive tape can be used to pick up small dust deposits.

Procedure

- Pick up or vacuum (see EM4 Using a Type H vacuum cleaner when working with asbestos) any bulk debris - see appropriate task guidance sheet.

- Soak rag in water and fold into half or quarters.

- Wring out and wipe contaminated surface.

- Do not soak again as this will contaminate the water.

- Refold rag to give clean surface.

- Repeat until all clean surfaces on the rag have been used.

- Repeat with a clean cloth until the surface is clean.

- Impregnated rags do not need to be soaked in water.

- If using tape, place a strip over the contaminated surface and slowly remove.

- Dispose of the dirty tape and repeat with a fresh piece.

- Tape is only appropriate for small dust deposits. Surfaces may need to be wiped again using the above method.

Waste disposal

- Place used rags and tape in a suitable asbestos waste container.

- As long as dirty rags are not soaked during cleaning, no special precautions need to be taken for disposal of water.

REMEMBER TO READ THE SAFETY CHECKLIST

ASBESTOS GUIDANCE

Personal decontamination

Description

This guidance sheet explains how you should decontaminate yourself after working with asbestos materials.

If you do not decontaminate yourself properly you may take asbestos fibres home on your clothing. You or your family and friends could be exposed to them if they were disturbed and became airborne.

It is important that you follow the procedures given in the task guidance sheets and wear personal protective equipment (PPE) such as overalls correctly, this will make cleaning easier.

Removing and decontaminating PPE

- Remove your respirator last.

- Clean your boots with wet rags.

- Where available, use a Type H vacuum cleaner to clean your overalls.

- Otherwise use a wet rag - use a 'patting' action - rubbing can disturb fibres.

Figure 15 'Buddy' cleaning using a Type H vacuum cleaner

- Where two or more workers are involved they can help each other by 'buddy' cleaning (Figure 15).

- Remove overalls by turning inside out - place in suitable asbestos waste container.

- Use wet rags to clean waterproof clothing.

- Disposable respirators can then be removed and placed in a suitable asbestos waste container.

Personal decontamination

- Site washing facilities can be used but restrict access during asbestos work.

- Wash each time you leave the work area.

- Use wet rags to clean washing facilities at the end of the job.

- Clean facilities daily if the job lasts more than one day.

- Visually inspect the facilities once the job is finished.

- Clearance air sampling is not normally required.

REMEMBER TO READ THE SAFETY CHECKLIST

ASBESTOS TASKS

A1
TASK GUIDANCE SHEET

Drilling holes in asbestos insulating board

Equipment

- 500 gauge poly-thene sheeting and duct tape.

- Warning tape and notices.

- A thick paste, eg wallpaper paste.

- Type H vacuum cleaner to BS5415.

- Drill - manual or power set at the lowest speed.

- Drill bit - use a hole cutter for holes greater than 20 mm.

- Plastic 'enclosure' to allow vacuum cleaner nozzle to provide extraction around drill bit.

- Sealant, select one low in hazardous constituents eg solvents.

- Plastic or metal sleeve.

- Bucket of water and rags.

- Suitable asbestos waste container, eg a labelled poly-thene sack.

- Appropriate lighting.

Description

This task guidance sheet can be used where asbestos insulating board (AIB) needs to be drilled to allow fittings to be attached, cables and pipework to be passed through walls etc. Two methods are given:

Method 1 - One to five holes up to 20 mm in diameter in board less than 6 mm thick;

Method 2 - Six to twenty holes, or any hole greater than 20 mm in diameter, or if drilling through board greater than 6 mm thick.

Only carry out this work if you are properly trained. See EM2 - Training.

Personal protective equipment (PPE)

- Disposable overalls fitted with a hood.

- Boots without laces (laced boots can be difficult to clean).

- Disposable particulate respirator (FF P3).

Preparing the work area

This work may be carried out at height, if so, the appropriate precautions to prevent a risk of falls MUST be taken.

- Carry out the work with the minimum number of people present.

- Restrict access, eg close the door and/or use warning tape and notices.

- If access is available to the rear of the AIB, segregate as above.

- If access cannot be gained to the rear, tell your supervisor/building manager - this can then be noted.

- Use polythene sheeting, secured with duct tape, to cover any surface within the segregated area which could become contaminated.

- Ensure adequate lighting.

Drilling - general preparation

- Cover the point to be drilled and rear, if accessible, with duct tape to prevent the edges crumbling.

- If cable or pipework is to be passed through, make sure the hole is slightly bigger to prevent abrasion.

REMEMBER TO READ THE SAFETY CHECKLIST

Method 1

- Cover the entry and exit points (if accessible) with a generous amount of paste.

- Drill through the paste (Figure 16).

- Use wet rags to clean off the paste and debris. Clean back of board if accessible.

- Dispose of as asbestos waste as this will contain dust and fibres.

- Seal drilled edge with sealant and insert sleeve as this will protect the inner edge of the hole.

Figure 16 Drilling through paste

Method 2

- Place the plastic 'enclosure' over the drill hole and place drill bit or hole cutter in opening.

- Attach Type H vacuum cleaner to plastic enclosure and switch on.

- Drill the hole (Figure 17).

- Vacuum the drill hole, including the rear if accessible.

Figure 17 Drilling through plastic enclosure

- Seal drilled edge with sealant and insert sleeve as this will protect the inner edge of the hole.

Cleaning

- Use wet rags and/or the Type H vacuum to clean the equipment.

- Use and wet rags and/or the Type H vacuum to clean the segregated area.

- Place used rags, polythene sheeting and other waste in the waste container.

Personal decontamination

- Use EM8 - Personal decontamination.

Clearance procedure

- Visually inspect the area to make sure that it has been properly cleaned.

- Clearance air sampling is not normally required.

What you need to read

- *Safety of electrical motor-operated industrial and commercial cleaning appliances. Particular requirements. Specification for vacuum cleaners, wet and/or dry* BS 5415 2.2 Supplement No 1: 1986
- *Tower scaffolds* Construction Information Sheet CIS10 HSE Books 1997
- *General access scaffolds and ladders* Construction Information Sheet CIS49 HSE Books 1997
- EM1 - What to do if you uncover asbestos materials or they are damaged
- EM2 - Training
- EM4 - Using a Type H vacuum cleaner when working with asbestos
- EM6 - Personal protective equipment
- EM7 - Using rags to clean surfaces and equipment contaminated with asbestos
- EM8 - Personal decontamination

A1

TASK GUIDANCE SHEET

REMEMBER TO READ THE SAFETY CHECKLIST

ASBESTOS TASKS

Removal of a single asbestos insulating board ceiling tile

Equipment

- Method 1 - 500 gauge polythene sheeting.

- Method 2 - proprietary 'mini-enclosure' or timber or other framework, 1000 gauge polythene sheeting, duct and masking tape.

- Warning tape and notices.

- Type H vacuum cleaner to BS5415.

- Magnet and screwdriver.

- Sealant eg polyvinyl acetate (PVA)

- Bucket of water, garden type spray and rags.

- Asbestos warning stickers.

- Suitable asbestos waste container, eg a labelled polythene sack.

- Non-asbestos replacement ceiling tile.

- Appropriate lighting.

Description

This task guidance sheet can be used where a single asbestos insulating board (AIB) ceiling tile needs to be removed). Two methods are given:

Method 1: removing a single ceiling tile less than 0.36 m^2 (eg 60 cms x 60 cms) in area.

Method 2: removing a single ceiling tile more than 0.36 m^2 (eg 60 cms x 60 cms) in area.

It is not appropriate:

- for the removal of AIB ceiling slats;

- where the ceiling tiles have more than minor damage;

- for heavily painted tiles that may damage adjacent tiles on removal.

Use a specialist contractor licensed by HSE for the above situations.

Only carry out this work if you are properly trained. See EM2 - Training.

Personal protective equipment (PPE)

- Disposable overalls fitted with a hood.

- Boots without laces (laced boots can be difficult to decontaminate).

- Disposable particulate respirator (FF P3).

General preparation

This work may be carried out at height, if so, the appropriate precautions to prevent a risk of falls MUST be taken.

- Carry out the work with the minimum number of people present.

- Restrict access, eg close the door and/or use warning tape and notices.

- Where necessary erect access platform.

- Ensure adequate lighting.

Method 1

- A 'mini-enclosure' is not normally required.

- Use 500 gauge polythene sheeting and duct tape to cover surfaces within the segregated area which could become contaminated.

REMEMBER TO READ THE SAFETY CHECKLIST

Method 2

- If available, erect a proprietary 'mini-enclosure'.

- Alternatively, use timber or other framework, polythene sheeting and tape to build a 'mini-enclosure' (EM3 Building a 'mini-enclosure' for the removal of a single asbestos insulating board ceiling tile).

Method 1 and 2 - Tile removal

- Use magnet to locate screws.

- Unscrew using shadow vacuuming.

- For brass screws locate by carefully scraping paint using shadow vacuuming.

- Carefully lower one end of the tile and vacuum upper surface (Figure 18).

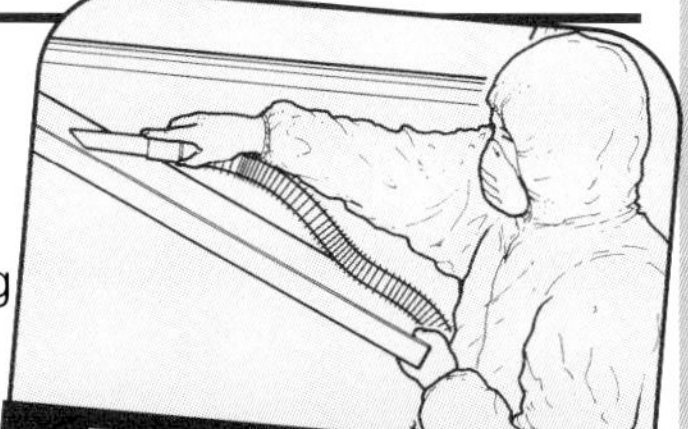

Figure 18 Vacuuming the back of the tile

- Lower the tile and spray upper surface with PVA (Figure 19).

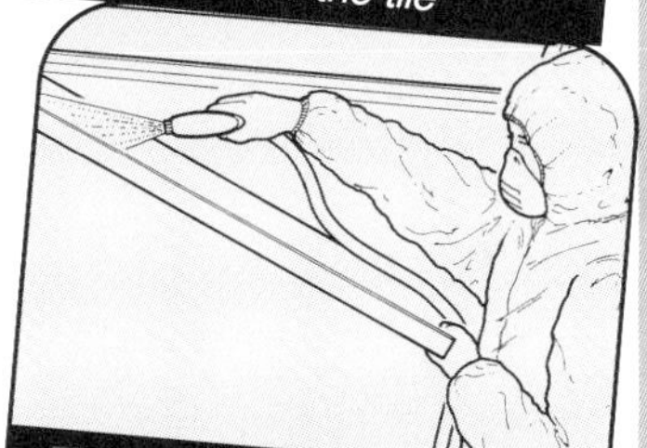

- Keeping the tile flat, lower and double wrap in 1000 gauge polythene sheeting and attach asbestos warning stickers.

- Small ceiling tiles can be placed in the waste container.

Figure 19 Spraying the back of a tile with PVA

- If asbestos fillets are present, seal with a sealant.

- Replace tile with a suitable non-asbestos type by attaching to non-asbestos surface rather than asbestos fillets.

Cleaning

- Using the Type H vacuum cleaner, clean enclosure/segregated area.

- Use wet rags to wipe clean the equipment.

- Dismantle the enclosure (see EM3 Building a 'mini-enclosure' for the removal of a single asbestos insulating board ceiling tile).

- Place used rags, polythene sheeting and other waste in the waste container.

Personal decontamination

Use EM8 - Personal decontamination.

Clearance procedure

- Visually inspect the area to make sure that it has been properly cleaned.

- Clearance air sampling is not normally required.

What you need to read

- *Tower scaffolds* Construction Information Sheet CIS10 HSE Books 1997
- *General access scaffolds and ladders* Construction Information Sheet CIS49 HSE Books 1997
- EM1 - What to do if you uncover asbestos materials or they are damaged during the task
- EM2 - Training
- EM3 - Building a 'mini-enclosure' for the removal of a single asbestos insulating board ceiling tile'
- EM4 - Using a Type H vacuum cleaner when working with asbestos
- EM5 - Wetting asbestos materials
- EM6 - Personal protective equipment
- EM7 - Using rags to clean surfaces and equipment contaminated with asbestos
- EM8 - Personal decontamination

A2

TASK GUIDANCE SHEET

REMEMBER TO READ THE SAFETY CHECKLIST

29

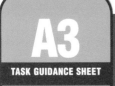

Removal of a door with asbestos insulating board fireproofing

Equipment

- 1000 gauge polythene sheeting and duct tape.

- Warning tape and notices.

- Sealant, eg polyvinyl acetate (PVA).

- Bucket of water, garden type spray and rags.

- Asbestos warning stickers.

- Appropriate lighting.

Description

This task guidance sheet can be used where a door backed with asbestos insulating board (AIB) needs to be disposed of (Figure 20). It can also be used where the AIB is sandwiched within the door.

It is not appropriate;

- for the removal of an AIB panel from a door. (Use A4 Removal of single screwed in asbestos insulating board less than 1 m² in area);

- the disposal of a door with more than minor damage to the AIB.

Use a specialist contractor licensed by HSE in each of these situations.

Only carry out this work if you are properly trained. See EM2 - Training.

Personal protective equipment (PPE)

- Disposable overalls fitted with a hood.

- Boots without laces (laced boots can be difficult to clean).

- Disposable particle respirator (FF P3)

Preparing the work area

- Carry out the work with the minimum number of people present.

- Restrict access, eg close the door and/or use warning tape and notices.

- Ensure adequate lighting.

Figure 20 Door with AIB panel

Removal

- If unpainted, spray the board with PVA sealant and allow to dry.

- If the board is within the door, spray any exposed edges.

- Lay polythene sheeting on the floor - large enough to wrap the door.

- Unscrew the hinges.

- Carefully lower onto the polythene sheet.

- Double wrap the door in polythene sheeting and secure with duct tape (Figure 21).

- Label package with asbestos warning stickers.

- If necessary, replace with a door with the same fire protection properties.

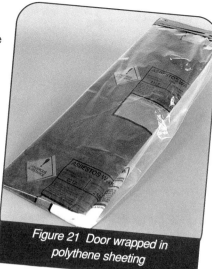

Figure 21 Door wrapped in polythene sheeting

What you need to read

- EM1 - What to do if you uncover asbestos materials or they are damaged during the task
- EM2 - Training
- EM5 - Wetting asbestos materials
- EM6 - Personal protective equipment
- EM7 - Using rags to clean surfaces and equipment contaminated with asbestos
- EM8 - Personal decontamination

Cleaning

- Use wet rags to clean the equipment.

- Place debris, used rags, polythene sheeting and other waste in the waste container.

Personal decontamination

- Use EM8 - Personal decontamination.

Clearance procedure

- Visually inspect the area to make sure that it has been properly cleaned.

- Clearance air sampling is not normally required.

A3

TASK GUIDANCE SHEET

REMEMBER TO READ THE SAFETY CHECKLIST

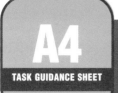

ASBESTOS TASKS

Removal of a single screwed in asbestos insulating board under 1 m² in area

Equipment

- 500 and 1000 gauge polythene sheeting and duct tape.

- Warning tape and notices.

- Type H vacuum cleaner to BS5415.

- Magnet and screwdriver.

- Sealant, eg polyvinyl acetate(PVA).

- Bucket of water, garden type spray and rags.

- Asbestos warning stickers.

- Suitable asbestos waste container, eg a labelled polythene sack.

- Appropriate lighting.

Description

This task guidance sheet can be used where a single asbestos insulating board (AIB) less than 1m² in area, needs to be removed (Figure 22).

It is not appropriate where:

- the AIB panel is nailed in place;

- the AIB has more than minor damage;

- the AIB is heavily painted and removal could damage adjacent panelling;

- the AIB is in the form of ceiling tiles or slats.

Figure 22 Asbestos insulating board wall panels

Use a specialist contractor licensed by HSE in each of the above situations.

Only carry out this work if you are properly trained. See EM2 - Training.

Personal protective equipment (PPE)

- Disposable overalls fitted with a hood.

- Boots without laces (laced boots can be difficult to clean).

- Disposable particulate respirator (FF P3).

Preparing the work area

This work may be carried out at height, if so, the appropriate precautions to prevent the risk of falls MUST be taken.

- Carry out the work with the minimum number of people present.

- Restrict access, eg close the door and/or use warning tape and notices.

- Where necessary, erect access platform.

REMEMBER TO READ THE SAFETY CHECKLIST

- Inspect the boards. If in good condition, firmly attached and unlikely to be damaged follow this task guidance sheet. If the boards are, or likely to be damaged use a specialist contractor licensed by HSE.

- Use 500 gauge polythene sheeting, secured with duct tape, to cover surfaces within the segregated area which could become contaminated.

- Ensure adequate lighting.

Removal

- Use magnet to locate screws.

- Unscrew using shadow vacuuming (Figure 23).

- For brass screws locate by carefully scraping paint using shadow vacuuming .

- Carefully ease back one end of the panel and vacuum the back surface.

- Spray the back surface with PVA.

- Remove all screws in the same way and lower the board.

- Place in the waste container or double wrap panel in 1000 polythene sheeting and attach asbestos warning stickers.

Figure 23 Shadow vacuuming during unscrewing

Cleaning

- Use the Type H vacuum cleaner to clean the framework.

- Use a screwdriver and Type H vacuum cleaner to clean the screw holes.

- Use the Type H vacuum and wet rags to clean the segregated area.

- Use the Type H vacuum and wet rags to clean the equipment.

- Place debris, used rags, polythene sheeting and other waste in the waste container.

Personal decontamination

- Use EM8 - Personal decontamination.

Clearance procedure

- Visually inspect the area to make sure that it has been properly cleaned.

- Clearance air sampling is not normally required.

What you need to read

- *Safety of electrical motor-operated industrial and commercial clean ing appliances. Particular require ments. Specification for vacuum cleaners, wet and/or dry BS 5415 2.2 Supplement No 1: 1986*
- *Tower scaffolds* Construction Information Sheet CIS10 HSE Books 1997
- *General access scaffolds and ladders* Construction Information Sheet CIS49 HSE Books 1997
- EM1 - What to do if you uncover asbestos materials or they are damaged during the task
- EM2 - Training
- EM4 - Using a Type H vacuum cleaner when working with asbestos
- EM5 - Wetting asbestos materials
- EM6 - Personal protective equipment
- EM7 - Using rags to clean surfaces and equipment contaminated with asbestos
- EM8 - Personal decontamination

A4

TASK GUIDANCE SHEET

REMEMBER TO READ THE SAFETY CHECKLIST

A5

TASK GUIDANCE SHEET

Cleaning light fittings attached to asbestos insulating board

Equipment

- 500 gauge polythene sheeting and duct tape.

- Warning tape and notices.

- Type H vacuum cleaner to BS5415.

- Bucket of water and rags.

- Suitable asbestos waste container, eg a labelled polythene sack.

- Appropriate lighting.

Description

This task guidance sheet can be used where it is necessary to clean a contaminated light fitting attached to asbestos insulating board (AIB) before carrying out work, eg changing a bulb.

It is not applicable if then AIB is damaged or likely to be damaged, eg by 'rocking' the screws during cleaning. Use a specialist contractor licensed by HSE.

Only carry out this work if you are properly trained. See EM2 - Training.

Personal protective equipment (PPE)

- Disposable overalls fitted with a hood.

- Boots without laces (laced boots can be difficult to clean).

- Disposable particulate respirator (FF P3).

Preparing the work area

This work may be carried out at height, if so, the appropriate precautions to prevent a risk of falls MUST be taken.

- Carry out the work with the minimum number of people present.

- Restrict access, eg close the door and/or use warning tape and notices.

- Use polythene sheeting, secured with duct tape, to cover surfaces within the segregated area which could become contaminated.

- Ensure adequate lighting.

Cleaning

- Ensure the power is isolated.

- Avoid removing the light fitting as this may disturb the AIB.

REMEMBER TO READ THE SAFETY CHECKLIST

- Use the Type H vacuum cleaner to clean the outside of the light fitting.

- Open the light fitting carefully and wide enough to insert the hose from the Type H vacuum to clean inside the fitting.

- Easily removable sections can be placed on polythene sheeting and cleaned on the floor (Figure 24).

Figure 24 Vacuuming light fitting housing

- Use the Type H vacuum cleaner to complete cleaning of the light fitting (Figure 25).

- Use wet rags to clean the segregated area.

- Place debris, used rags, polythene sheeting and other waste in the waste container.

Personal decontamination

- Use EM8 - Personal decontamination.

Figure 25 Vacuuming light fitting

Clearance procedure

- Visually inspect the area to make sure that it has been properly cleaned.

- Clearance air sampling is not normally required.

What you need to read

- *Safety of electrical motor-operated industrial and commercial cleaning appliances. Particular requirements. Specification for vacuum cleaners, wet and/or dry* BS 5415 2.2 Supplement No 1: 1986
- *Tower scaffolds* Construction Information Sheet CIS10 HSE Books 1997
- *General access scaffolds and ladders* Construction Information Sheet CIS49 HSE Books 1997
- EM1 - What to do if you uncover asbestos materials or they are damaged during the task
- EM2 - Training
- EM4 - Using a Type H vacuum cleaner when working with asbestos
- EM6 - Personal protective equipment
- EM7 - Using rags to clean surfaces and equipment contaminated with asbestos
- EM8 - Personal decontamination

A5

TASK GUIDANCE SHEET

REMEMBER TO READ THE SAFETY CHECKLIST

ASBESTOS TASKS

Repairing minor damage to asbestos insulating board

Equipment

- 500 gauge polythene sheeting and duct tape.

- Warning tape and notices.

- Non-asbestos panelling.

- Liquid nails (Figure 26).

- Paint conforming to the original specification, eg fire resistant. Select one low in hazardous constituents, eg solvents.

- Bucket of water and rags.

- Garden type spray or small paint brush.

- Suitable asbestos waste container, eg a labelled polythene sack.

- Appropriate lighting.

Description

This task guidance sheet can be used where small areas of damaged asbestos insulating board need to be repaired eg a broken corner, scratches etc.

It is not appropriate where the material is badly damaged. Use a specialist contractor licensed by HSE.

Only carry out this work if you are properly trained. See EM2 - Training.

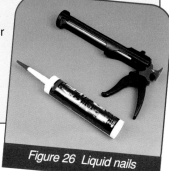

Figure 26 Liquid nails

Personal protective equipment (PPE)

- Disposable overalls fitted with a hood.

- Boots without laces (laced boots can be difficult to decontaminate).

- Disposable particulate respirator (FF P3).

Preparing the work area

This work may be carried out at height, if so, the appropriate precautions to prevent a risk of falls MUST be taken.

- Carry out the work with the minimum number of people present.

- Restrict access, eg the close door and/or use warning tape and notices.

- Use polythene sheeting, secured with duct tape, to cover surfaces within the segregated area which may become contaminated

- Ensure adequate lighting.

REMEMBER TO READ THE SAFETY CHECKLIST

Repair

■ Use a wet rag to remove small bits of loose board.

■ Place in the waste container.

■ Use spray or paint brush to paint the damaged area.

■ Cover holes with non-asbestos panel attached with liquid nails (Figure 27) - if necessary use wet rag to remove any dirt or dust.

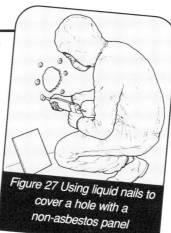

Figure 27 Using liquid nails to cover a hole with a non-asbestos panel

Cleaning

■ Use wet rags to clean the equipment.

■ Use wet rags to clean the segregated area.

■ Place debris, used rags, polythene sheeting and other waste in the waste container.

Personal decontamination

■ Use EM8 - Personal decontamination.

Clearance procedure

■ Visually inspect the area to make sure that it has been properly cleaned.

■ Clearance air sampling is not normally required.

What you need to read

■ *Tower scaffolds* Construction Information Sheet CIS10 HSE Books 1997
■ *General access scaffolds and ladders* Construction Information Sheet CIS49 HSE Books 1997
■ EM1 - What to do if you uncover asbestos materials or they are damaged during the task
■ EM2 - Training
■ EM6 - Personal protective equipment
■ EM7 - Using rags to clean surfaces and equipment contaminated with asbestos
■ EM8 - Personal decontamination

A6

TASK GUIDANCE SHEET

REMEMBER TO READ THE SAFETY CHECKLIST

A7

Painting undamaged asbestos insulating board

Equipment

- 500 gauge polythene sheeting and duct tape.

- Warning tape and notices.

- Type H vacuum cleaner to BS5415 (if dust needs to be removed from the asbestos insulating board).

- Paint conforming to the original specification, eg fire resistant. Select one low in hazardous constituents, eg solvents.

- Low pressure spray or roller/brush.

- Bucket of water and rags.

- Suitable asbestos waste container eg a labelled polythene sack.

- Appropriate lighting.

Description

This task guidance sheet can be used where undamaged asbestos insulating board needs to be painted (Figure 28). This may be to protect them, or for aesthetic reasons.

It is not appropriate where the material is damaged. Use a specialist contractor licensed by HSE.

Only carry out this work if you are properly trained. See EM2 - Training.

Figure 28 Painted ceiling tiles in a corridor

Personal protective equipment (PPE)

- Disposable overalls fitted with a hood.

- Boots without laces (laced boots can be difficult to decontaminate).

- Disposable particulate respirator (FF P3).

Preparing the work area

- This work may be carried out at height, if so, the appropriate precautions MUST be taken.

- Carry out the work with the minimum number of people present.

- Restrict access, eg close the door and/or use warning tape and notices.

- Use polythene sheeting, secured with duct tape, to cover surfaces within the segregated area which could become contaminated.

- Ensure adequate lighting.

REMEMBER TO READ THE SAFETY CHECKLIST

Painting

- Never prepare surfaces by sanding.

- Before starting, check there is no damage.

- Repair any minor damage (see A6, Repairing minor damage to asbestos insulating board).

- If dust needs to be removed, use a Type H vacuum cleaner or rags.

Figure 29 Spraying paint onto asbestos insulating board

- Preferably use the spray to apply the paint (Figure 29).

- Spray using a sweeping motion.

- Do not concentrate on one area as this could cause damage.

- Alternatively, apply the brush/roller lightly to avoid abrasion/damage.

Cleaning

- Use wet rags to clean the equipment.

- Use wet rags to clean the segregated area.

- Place debris, used rags, polythene sheeting and other waste in the waste container.

Personal decontamination

- Use EM8 - Personal decontamination.

Clearance procedure

- Visually inspect the area to make sure that it has been properly cleaned.

- Clearance air sampling is not normally required.

What you need to read

- *Safety of electrical motor-operated industrial and commercial clean ing appliances. Particular require ments. Specification for vacuum cleaners, wet and/or dry* BS 5415 2.2 Supplement No 1: 1986
- *General access scaffolds and ladders* Construction Information Sheet CIS49 HSE Books 1997
- EM1 - What to do if you uncover asbestos materials or they are damaged during the task
- EM2 - Training
- EM4 - Using a Type H vacuum cleaner when work ing with asbestos
- EM5 - Wetting asbestos materials
- EM6 - Personal protective equipment
- EM7 - Using rags to clean surfaces and equipment contaminated with asbestos
- EM8 - Personal decontamination

A7

TASK GUIDANCE SHEET

ASBESTOS TASKS

Enclosing undamaged asbestos materials to prevent impact damage

Equipment

- Warning tape and notices.

- Non-asbestos boarding (this may need to be the original specification, eg fire protection).

- Liquid nails (Figure 30).

- Nails or screws.

- Bucket of water and rags.

- Suitable asbestos waste container, eg a labelled polythene sack.

- Appropriate lighting.

Description

This task guidance sheet can be used where undamaged asbestos materials need to be protected from impact damage and you do not want to remove them.

For example; asbestos insulating board wall panels which could be damaged by trolleys in a hospital, or lagged pipework running along the bottom of a wall which could be scuffed.

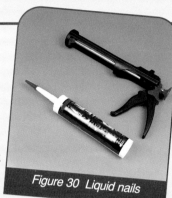

Figure 30 Liquid nails

It is not appropriate where the asbestos material is damaged.

Only carry out this work if you are properly trained. See EM2 - Training.

Personal protective equipment

- Disposable overalls fitted with a hood.

- Boots without laces (laced boots can be difficult to decontaminate).

- A respirator will not normally be required if this procedure is followed. But, a disposable particulate respirator (FF P3) can be used if reassurance is needed.

Preparing the work area

- Carry out the work with the minimum number of people present.

- Restrict access, eg close the door and/or use warning tape and notices.

- Ensure adequate lighting.

Enclosing the asbestos material

■ Repair any minor areas of damage to asbestos insulating board or asbestos cement (See A6 - Repairing minor damage to asbestos insulating board or A13 - Repairing damaged asbestos cement).

■ Repairs to asbestos lagging or coatings must be carried out by a specialist contractor licensed by HSE.

■ Where possible, fix non-asbestos panels (covering the asbestos material) to non-asbestos materials - nails or screws can then be used.

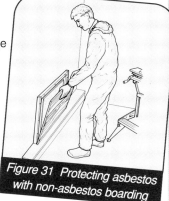

Figure 31 Protecting asbestos with non-asbestos boarding

■ Pipework can be boxed in without disturbing the lagging.

■ If necessary, use liquid nails to attach non-asbestos panels to asbestos insulating board (Figure 31) – do not use on asbestos cement.

■ Seal cavity and provide adequate fire barriers.

■ Note the presence of asbestos material so that it can be managed.

Cleaning

■ Use wet rags to clean the equipment.

■ Use wet rags to clean the segregated area.

■ Place debris, used rags and other waste in the waste container.

Personal decontamination

■ Use EM8 - Personal decontamination.

Clearance procedure

■ Visually inspect the area to make sure that it has been properly cleaned.

■ Clearance air sampling is not normally required.

What you need to read

■ EM1 - What to do if you uncover asbestos materials or they are damaged during the task
■ EM2 - Training
■ EM6 - Personal protective equipment
■ EM7 - Using rags to clean surfaces and equipment contaminated with asbestos
■ EM8 - Personal decontamination

A8

TASK GUIDANCE SHEET

REMEMBER TO READ THE SAFETY CHECKLIST

A9

Drilling holes in asbestos cement and other highly bonded materials

Equipment

- 500 gauge polythene sheeting and duct tape.

- Warning tape and notices.

- A thick paste, eg wallpaper paste.

- Drill - manual or power set at the lowest speed.

- Drill bit - use a hole cutter for larger holes.

- Sealant, eg alkali resistant and vapour permeable – select one low in hazardous constituents.

- Plastic or metal sleeve.

- Bucket of water and rags.

- Suitable asbestos waste container, eg a labelled polythene sack.

- Appropriate lighting.

Description

This task guidance sheet can be used where holes need to be drilled in asbestos cement, decorative coatings, bitumen products containing asbestos, floor tiles and other highly bonded materials containing asbestos.

Task guidance sheet A1 - Drilling holes in asbestos insulating board should be used when drilling holes in asbestos insulating board.

Only carry out this work if you are properly trained.
See EM2 - Training.

Personal protective equipment (PPE)

- Disposable overalls fitted with a hood.

- Waterproof overalls may be required outside.

- Boots without laces (laced boots can be difficult to decontaminate).

- Disposable particulate respirator (FF P3).

Preparing the work area

This work may be carried out at height, if so, the appropriate precautions to prevent the risk of falls MUST be taken.

- Carry out the work with the minimum number of people present.

- Restrict access, eg close door and/or use warning tape and notices.

- If drilling a roof from outside, segregate the area below.

- If access is available to the rear of the asbestos cement, segregate as above.

- If access cannot be gained to the rear, tell your supervisor/building manager so this can be noted.

- Use polythene sheeting, secured with duct tape, to cover any surface within the segregated area which could become contaminated.

- Ensure adequate lighting.

REMEMBER TO READ THE SAFETY CHECKLIST

Drilling

- Cover the point to be drilled and rear if accessible, with tape to prevent the edges crumbling.

- If cable or pipework is to be passed through, make sure the hole is slightly bigger to prevent abrasion.

- Cover the entry and exit points (if accessible) with a generous amount of paste.

Figure 32 Drilling through paste

- Drill through the paste (Figure 32).

- Use wet rags to clean off the paste and debris.

- Include accessible surfaces at the rear.

- Dispose of as asbestos waste as this will contain dust and fibres.

- Seal cut edges with sealant.

- If a cable is to be passed through, insert a sleeve to protect the inner edge of the hole

Cleaning

- Use wet rags to clean the equipment.

- Use wet rags to clean the segregated area.

- Place debris, used rags, polythene sheeting and other waste in the waste container.

Personal decontamination

- Use EM8 - Personal decontamination.

Clearance procedure

- Visually inspect the area to make sure that it has been properly cleaned.

- Clearance air sampling is not normally required.

What you need to read

- *Tower scaffolds* Construction Information Sheet CIS10 HSE Books 1997
- *General access scaffolds and ladders* Construction Information Sheet CIS49 HSE Books 1997
- EM1 - What to do if you uncover asbestos materials or they are damaged during the task
- EM2 - Training
- EM6 - Personal protective equipment
- EM7 - Using rags to clean surfaces and equipment contaminated with asbestos
- EM8 - Personal decontamination

TASK
A9
TASK GUIDANCE SHEET

REMEMBER TO READ THE SAFETY CHECKLIST

ASBESTOS TASKS

Cleaning debris from guttering
on an asbestos cement roof

Equipment

- Access platform, eg scaffolding.

- Warning tapes and notices.

- Bucket of water and detergent.

- Watering can or garden type spray.

- Scoop or trowel.

- Rags.

- Suitable asbestos waste container, eg a labelled polythene sack.

Description

This task guidance sheet can be used where debris containing asbestos needs to be removed from guttering (this can be made from asbestos cement or other non-asbestos material) on an asbestos cement roof.

Only carry out this work if you are properly trained. See EM2 – Training.

Personal protective equipment (PPE)

- Disposable overalls fitted with a hood.

- Waterproof overalls may be required outside.

- Boots without laces (laced boots can be difficult to decontaminate).

- A respirator will not normally be required if this procedure is followed. But, a disposable particulate respirator (FF P3) can be used if reassurance is needed.

Preparing the work area

This work may be carried out at height, if so, the appropriate precautions to prevent the risk of falls MUST be taken.

- Carry out the work with the minimum number of people present.

- Restrict access, eg use warning tapes and notices.

- Erect access platform.

Gutter cleaning

- Mix water and detergent.

- Using the watering (or garden type spray), pour water into the gutter but avoid over wetting as this will create a slurry.

- Remove debris using the scoop or trowel (Figure 33).

- Wet the debris again if dry material is uncovered.

- Place debris straight into the waste container.

Cleaning

- Use wet rags to clean the equipment.

- Use wet rags to clean the access platform.

- Place debris, used rags, and other waste in the waste container.

Figure 33 Cleaning guttering

Personal decontamination

- Use EM8 - Personal decontamination.

Clearance procedure

- Visually inspect the platform and surrounding area to make sure that it has been properly cleaned.

- Clearance air sampling is not normally required.

What you need to read

- *Health and safety in roof work* HSG33 HSE Books 1998 ISBN 0 7176 1425 5
- *Tower scaffolds* Construction Information Sheet CIS10 HSE Books 1997
- *General access scaffolds and ladders* Construction Information Sheet CIS49 HSE Books 1997
- EM1 - What to do if you uncover asbestos materials or they are damaged during the task
- EM2 - Training
- EM5 - Wetting asbestos materials
- EM6 - Personal protective equipment
- EM7 - Using rags to clean surfaces and equipment contaminated with asbestos
- EM8 - Personal decontamination

A10
TASK GUIDANCE SHEET

REMEMBER TO READ THE SAFETY CHECKLIST

A11
TASK GUIDANCE SHEET

Removal of asbestos cement debris

Equipment

- Warning tape and notices.

- Bucket of water, garden type spray and rags.

- Suitable asbestos waste container, eg a labelled polythene sack.

- Appropriate lighting.

Description

This task guidance sheet can be used where there is contamination from damaged asbestos cement. This includes decontamination work following the rupture of asbestos cement cladding in a fire. It is not appropriate for cleaning debris from damaged asbestos lagging, coating or insulating board.

Only carry out this work if you are properly trained. See EM2 – Training.

Personal protective equipment

- Disposable overalls fitted with a hood.

- Waterproof overalls may be required outside.

- Boots without laces (laced boots can be difficult to decontaminate).

- Disposable particulate respirator (FF P3).

- A respirator may not be required where the contamination is confined to a few pieces in a small area or it is already wet.

Preparing the work area

This work may be carried out at height, if so, the appropriate precautions to prevent the risk of falls MUST be taken.

- Carry out the work with the minimum number of people present.

- Restrict access, eg close door and/use warning tape and notices.

- Ensure adequate lighting.

Decontamination

- Use the spray to dampen the debris.

- Pick up larger pieces of debris and place in the waste container.

- In small areas, use wet rags to wipe clean contaminated surfaces. (Figure 34).

- In large areas eg following rupturing of asbestos cement in a fire, it is not always practical to wipe all surfaces, so restrict cleaning to obvious contamination in occupied areas eg windows.

- If the contaminated surface is rough, keep the debris damp and scrape into a waste container.

- Tape can be pressed onto dust deposits to pick them up.

- If necessary repair the asbestos cement (see A13 - Repairing damaged asbestos cement).

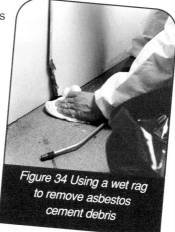

Figure 34 Using a wet rag to remove asbestos cement debris

Cleaning

Place used rags and other waste in the waste container.

Personal decontamination

Use EM8 - Personal decontamination.

Clearance procedure

- Visually inspect the area to make sure that it has been properly cleaned.

- Clearance air sampling is not normally required.

What you need to read

- *Health and safety in roof work* HSG33 HSE Books 1998 ISBN 0 7176 1425 5
- *Tower scaffolds* Construction Information Sheet CIS10 HSE Books 1997
- *General access scaffolds and ladders* Construction Information Sheet CIS49 HSE Books 1997
- EM1 - What to do if you uncover asbestos materials or they are damaged during the task
- EM2 - Training
- EM5 - Wetting asbestos materials
- EM6 - Personal protective equipment
- EM7 - Using rags to clean surfaces and equipment contaminated with asbestos
- EM8 - Personal decontamination

A11

TASK GUIDANCE SHEET

REMEMBER TO READ THE SAFETY CHECKLIST

ASBESTOS TASKS

A12
TASK GUIDANCE SHEET

Cleaning weathered asbestos cement roofing and cladding

Figure 35 Asbestos cement cladding showing moss and lichen growth

Equipment

- 500 gauge polythene sheeting and duct tape.

- Warning tape and notices.

- Approved pesticide (see Pesticides 2001 see opposite).

- Proprietary cleaning machine (Figure 36).

- Scraper.

- Bucket of water, garden type spray and rags.

- Suitable asbestos waste container eg labelled polythene sack.

- Appropriate lighting.

Figure 36 Cleaning machine

Description

This task guidance sheet can be used where weathered asbestos cement cladding and roofing needs to be cleaned. This may be for aesthetic reasons or before the application of a surface coating.

Moss and lichen growth (Figure 35) is normal. It may not be attractive, but it is unlikely to be detrimental and so unless there is a good reason for removal, it should be left in place. Two cleaning methods are given:

Method 1 - Cladding accessible from ground level.

Method 2 - Roofing - a specialist roof cleaning contractor will be needed.

This task guidance sheet is not appropriate for the cleaning of asbestos insulating board.

Only carry out this work if you are properly trained. See EM2 - Training.

Personal protective equipment

- Some biocides can irritate the skin, use protective gloves. Consult your supplier.

- Disposable overalls fitted with a hood.

- Waterproof clothing may be required outside.

- Boots without laces (laced boots can be difficult to decontaminate).

- As long as the worker operating the cleaning machine is remote from the unit, a respirator is not required.

- A disposable particulate respirator (FF P3) will be needed by workers operating the filtration system or scraping off growths.

Preparing the work area

This work may be carried out at height, if so, the appropriate precautions to prevent a risk of falls MUST be taken.

- Carry out the work with the minimum number of people present.

- Restrict access using warning tape.

- Use polythene sheeting secured with duct tape to seal gaps into the building to prevent slurry getting in.

- It is dangerous to seal over exhaust vents from heating units in use.

REMEMBER TO READ THE SAFETY CHECKLIST

Removal of growths - general

- High pressure jetting should only be used in exceptional circumstances by specialist contractors.

- If necessary remove any debris (use A11 - Removal of asbestos cement debris).

Method 1

- Prepare biocide to manufacturers' specification and apply using a low pressure spray.

- Allow sufficient time for biocide to kill growths. Remove growths by gentle scraping, keeping the asbestos cement wet. Dead roots can be difficult to remove and can be left in place.

- Place debris in the waste container.

Figure 37 Diverting slurry

Method 2

- This technique creates a lot of slurry. It must not enter the building and should be collected for disposal.

- Disconnect down pipes and divert slurry through a collection and filtration system (Figures 37 and 38).

- Solid waste should be kept wet and placed in a waste container.

- Follow manufacturers instructions to operate the cleaning machine.

Figure 38 Filtration unit

Cleaning (method 1 and 2)

- Method 2 - Use clean water to flush out the slurry collection system.

- Use wet rags to wipe clean the equipment.

- Use wet rags to clean the segregated area.

- Place used rags polythene sheeting and other waste in the waste container.

Personal decontamination

- Use EM8 - Personal decontamination.

Clearance procedure

- Visually inspect the area to make sure that it has been properly cleaned.

- Clearance air sampling is not normally required.

What you need to read

- *Health and safety in roof work* HSG33 HSE Books 1998 ISBN 0 7176 1425 5
- *Tower scaffolds* Construction Information Sheet CIS10 HSE Books 1997
- *General access scaffolds and ladders* Construction Information Sheet CIS49 HSE Books 1997
- *Pesticides 2001: Pesticides approved under the Control of Pesticide Regulations 1986 and the Plant Protection Products Regulations 1995* The Stationery Office 2001 ISBN 0 1124 3060 0
- EM1 - What to do if you uncover asbestos materials or they are damaged during the task
- EM2 - Training
- EM6 - Personal protective equipment
- EM7 - Using rags to clean surfaces and equipment contaminated with asbestos
- EM8 - Personal decontamination

A12
TASK GUIDANCE SHEET

A13
TASK GUIDANCE SHEET

Repairing damaged asbestos cement

Equipment

- 500 gauge polythene sheeting and duct tape.

- Warning tape and notices.

- Sealant, eg alkali resistant and vapour permeable – select one low in hazardous constituents eg solvents; and conforming to the original specification eg fire resistant.

- Bucket of water, garden type spray and rags.

- Suitable asbestos waste container, eg a labelled polythene sack.

- Appropriate lighting.

Description

This task guidance sheet can be used where damaged asbestos cement needs to be repaired.

It is not appropriate for the repair of asbestos insulating board.

Only carry out this work if you are properly trained. See EM2 - Training.

Personal protective equipment (PPE)

- Disposable overalls fitted with a hood.

- Waterproof clothing may be required outside.

- Boots without laces (laced boots can be difficult to decontaminate).

- A disposable particulate respirator (FF P3).

Preparing the work area

This work may be carried out at height, if so, the appropriate precautions to prevent a risk of falls MUST be taken.

- Carry out the work with the minimum number of people present.

- Restrict access, eg close door and/use warning tape and notices.

- Use polythene sheeting, secured with duct tape, to cover surfaces within the segregated area which could become contaminated.

- Ensure adequate lighting.

Repair

- If the asbestos cement is badly damaged, eg holes etc, remove the product (see A14 - Removal of asbestos cement sheets, gutters etc and/or A15 - Removal of asbestos cement products such as flues and tanks).

REMEMBER TO READ THE SAFETY CHECKLIST

- Clean up any debris and loose material (see A11 - Removal of asbestos cement debris).

- Paint damaged areas of asbestos cement (see A16 - Painting asbestos cement sheets) (Figure 39).

- Alternatively, protect asbestos cement by attaching non-asbestos panel over the asbestos cement (see A8 - Enclosing undamaged asbestos materials to prevent impact damage) (Figure 40).

- Note the presence of the asbestos cement so that it can be managed.

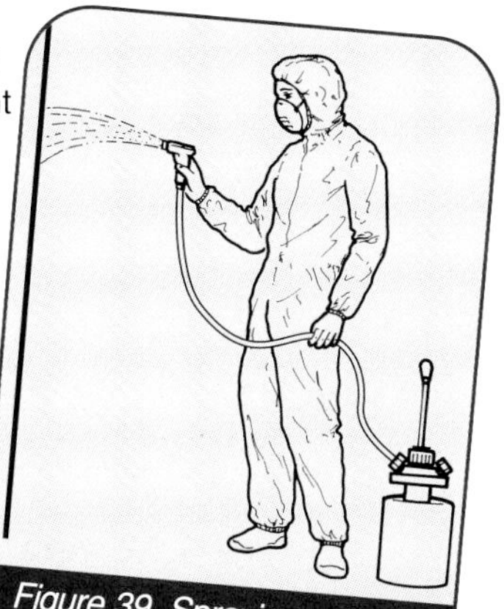

Figure 39 Spraying paint on asbestos cement

Cleaning

- Use wet rags to wipe clean the equipment.

- Use wet rags to wipe clean the segregated area.

- Place used rags, polythene sheeting and other waste in the waste container.

Figure 40 Protecting asbestos cement with non-asbestos boarding

Personal decontamination

- Use EM8 - Personal decontamination.

Clearance procedure

- Visually inspect the area to make sure that it has been properly cleaned.

- Clearance air sampling is not normally required.

What you need to read

- *Health and safety in roof work* HSG33 HSE Books 1998 ISBN 0 7176 1425 5
- *Tower scaffolds* Construction Information Sheet CIS10 HSE Books 1997
- *General access scaffolds and ladders* Construction Information Sheet CIS49 HSE Books 1997
- EM1 - What to do if you uncover asbestos materials or they are damaged during the task
- EM2 - Training
- EM5 - Wetting asbestos materials
- EM6 - Personal protective equipment
- EM7 - Using rags to clean surfaces and equipment contaminated with asbestos
- EM8 - Personal decontamination

A13
TASK GUIDANCE SHEET

REMEMBER TO READ THE SAFETY CHECKLIST

ASBESTOS TASKS

Removal of asbestos cement sheets, gutters etc

Equipment

■ 500 and 1000 gauge polythene sheeting and duct tape.

■ Warning tape and notices.

■ Bolt cutters.

■ Bucket of water, garden type spray and rags.

■ Suitable asbestos waste container, eg a labelled polythene sack.

■ Lockable skip for larger quantities of asbestos cement.

■ Asbestos warning stickers.

■ Appropriate lighting.

Description

This task guidance sheet can be used where asbestos cement sheets, gutters, drains and ridge caps etc need to be removed (Figure 41).

For the large scale removal of asbestos cement eg demolition, read *Working with asbestos cement* HSG189/2 HSE Books 1999 ISBN 0 7176 1667 3.

It is not appropriate for the removal of asbestos insulating board.

Only carry out this work if you are properly trained. See EM2 - Training.

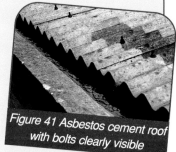

Figure 41 Asbestos cement roof with bolts clearly visible

Personal protective equipment (PPE)

■ Disposable overalls fitted with a hood.

■ Waterproof clothing may be required outside.

■ Boots without laces (laced boots can be difficult to decontaminate).

■ Disposable particulate respirator (FF P3).

Preparing the work area

This work may be carried out at height, if so, the appropriate precautions to prevent the risk of falls MUST be taken.

■ Carry out the work with the minimum number of people present.

■ Restrict access, eg close the door and/or use warning tape and notices.

■ Use 500 gauge polythene sheeting, secured with duct tape, to cover any surface within the segregated area which could become contaminated.

■ It is dangerous to seal over exhaust vents from heating units in use.

■ Ensure adequate lighting.

Overlaying

■ Instead of removing asbestos cement roofs, consider overlaying with a non-asbestos material.

REMEMBER TO READ THE SAFETY CHECKLIST

- Attach sheets to existing purlins but avoid drilling through the asbestos cement, otherwise use A9 'Drilling holes in asbestos cement and other highly bonded materials'.

- Note the presents of the asbestos cement so that it can be managed.

Removal

- Avoid breaking the asbestos cement products.

- If the sheets are held in place with fasteners, dampen and remove - take care not to create a risk of slips.

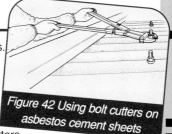

Figure 42 Using bolt cutters on asbestos cement sheets

- If the sheets are bolted in place, use bolt cutters avoiding contact with the asbestos cement. Remove bolts carefully (Figure 42).

- Unbolt or use bolt cutters to release gutters, drain pipes and ridge caps, avoiding contact with the asbestos cement.

- Lower the asbestos cement to the ground. Do not use rubble chutes.

- Check for debris in fasteners or bolt holes. Clean with wet rags.

- Single asbestos cement products can be double wrapped in 1000 gauge polythene sheeting (or placed in waste containers if small enough). Attach asbestos warning stickers.

- Where there are several asbestos cement sheets and other large items, place in a lockable skip.

Cleaning

- Use wet rags to clean the equipment.

- Use wet rags to clean segregated area.

- Place debris, used rags, polythene sheeting and other waste in the waste container.

Personal decontamination

- Use EM8 - Personal decontamination.

Clearance procedure

- Visually inspect the area to make sure that it has been properly cleaned.

- Clearance air sampling is not normally required.

What you need to read

- *Health and safety in roof work* HSG33 HSE Books 1998 ISBN 0 7176 1425 5
- EM1 - What to do if you uncover asbestos materials or they are damaged during the task
- EM2 - Training
- EM5 - Wetting asbestos materials
- EM6 - Personal protective equipment
- EM7 - Using rags to clean surfaces and equipment contaminated with asbestos
- EM8 - Personal decontamination

A14

TASK GUIDANCE SHEET

Removal of asbestos cement products such as flues and tanks

Equipment

- 500 and 1000 gauge polythene sheeting and duct tape.

- Warning tape and notices.

- Hammer.

- Bucket of water, garden type spray and rags.

- Suitable asbestos waste container, eg a labelled polythene sack.

- Asbestos warning stickers.

- Appropriate lighting.

Description

This task guidance sheet can be used where asbestos cement products such as flues, ventilation ducting and tanks need to removed from areas such as lofts (Figure 43).

It is not appropriate for work with asbestos insulating board.

If the asbestos cement product is no longer needed and will not interfere with any other installations/work then it is best to note its location and make sure it stays in good condition.

Only carry out this work if you are properly trained. See EM2 - Training.

Figure 43 Asbestos cement water tank

Personal protective equipment (PPE)

- Disposable overalls fitted with a hood.

- Boots without laces (laced boots can be difficult to decontaminate).

- Disposable particulate respirator (FF P3).

Preparing the work area

This work may be carried out at height, if so, the appropriate precautions MUST be taken.

- Carry out the work with the minimum number of people present.

- Restrict access, eg close the door, and/or use warning tape and notices.

- If the asbestos cement product is in an area like a loft, board out an area which can be worked on large enough to prevent contamination of adjacent loft insulation.

- Use 500 gauge polythene sheeting, secured with duct tape, to cover any surface within the segregated area which could become conaminated. (Avoid creating a risk of slips).

- Ensure adequate lighting.

Removal

■ Where possible minimise breakage of the asbestos cement.

■ If asbestos insulating board is present (eg on a flue) a specialist contractor licensed by HSE must do the work.

■ If it can be removed whole, strengthen damaged sections of asbestos cement with duct tape.

■ Where possible remove the asbestos cement product intact by unscrewing supports. If this is not possible, dampen the asbestos cement.

■ Wrap the asbestos cement in 1000 gauge polythene sheeting before breaking.

■ Using the hammer, carefully break the asbestos cement product into pieces small enough to be removed (Figure 44).

■ Place debris in the waste container.

■ Double wrap large items in 1000 gauge polythene sheeting and attach warning stickers.

Figure 44 Breaking asbestos cement

Cleaning

■ Use wet rags to clean the equipment.

■ Use wet rags to clean the segregated area.

■ Place debris, used rags, polythene sheeting and other waste in the waste container.

Personal decontamination

■ Use EM8 - Personal decontamination.

Clearance procedure

■ Visually inspect the area to make sure that it has been properly cleaned.

■ Clearance air sampling is not normally required.

What you need to read

■ *Tower scaffolds* Construction Information Sheet CIS10 HSE Books 1997
■ *General access scaffolds and ladders* Construction Information Sheet CIS49 HSE Books 1997
■ EM1 - What to do if you uncover asbestos materials or they are damaged during the task
■ EM2 - Training
■ EM5 - Wetting asbestos materials
■ EM6 - Personal protective equipment
■ EM7 - Using rags to clean surfaces and equipment contaminated with asbestos
■ EM8 - Personal decontamination

A15

TASK GUIDANCE SHEET

REMEMBER TO READ THE SAFETY CHECKLIST

A16

Painting asbestos cement sheets

Equipment

- 500 gauge polythene sheeting and duct tape.

- Warning tape and notices.

- Paint - alkali resistant and vapour permeable - select one low in hazardous constituents eg solvents.

- Low pressure spray or roller/brush.

- Bucket of water and rags.

- Suitable asbestos waste container, eg a labelled polythene sack.

- Appropriate lighting.

Description

This task guidance sheet can be used where asbestos cement in good condition, needs to be painted (Figure 45).

Note: if done wrong it can result in the sheets failing.

Asbestos cement sheets can be protected from impact damage using A8 - Enclosing undamaged asbestos materials to prevent impact damage.

If it is necessary to paint the asbestos cement follow this method.

Only carry out this work if you are properly trained. See EM2 - Training.

Figure 45 Unsealed Asbestos cement

Personal protective equipment (PPE)

- Disposable overalls fitted with a hood.

- Boots without laces (laced boots can be difficult to decontaminate).

- Disposable particulate respirator (FF P3).

Preparing the work area

This work may be carried out at height, if so, the appropriate precautions MUST be taken.

- Carry out the work with the minimum number of people present.

- Restrict access, eg close door and/or use warning tape and notices.

- Use polythene sheeting, secured with duct tape, to cover surfaces which could become contaminated.

- Ensure adequate lighting.

REMEMBER TO READ THE SAFETY CHECKLIST

Painting

- Never prepare surfaces by sanding.

- If lichen or other growths are present, remove (see A12 - Cleaning weathered asbestos cement roofing and cladding).

- Before starting, check the asbestos cement for damage and if necessary, repair (see A13 - Repairing damaged asbestos cement).

- Wipe dusty surfaces with a wet cloth.

- Preferably use a low pressure spray to apply the paint (Figure 46).

- Spray using a sweeping motion.

- Do not concentrate on one area as this could cause damage.

- Alternatively, use the brush/roller lightly to avoid abrasion/damage.

- Paint both sides of the sheet.

Cleaning

- Use wet rags to wipe clean the equipment.

- Use wet rags to wipe clean the segregated area.

Figure 46 Spraying paint onto asbestos cement

- Place debris, used rags, polythene sheeting and other waste in the waste container.

Personal decontamination

- Use EM8 - Personal decontamination.

Clearance procedure

- Visually inspect the area to make sure that it has been properly cleaned.

- Clearance air sampling is not normally required.

What you need to read

- *Tower scaffolds* Construction Information Sheet CIS10 HSE Books 1997
- *General access scaffolds and ladders* Construction Information Sheet CIS49 HSE Books 1997
- EM1 - What to do if you uncover asbestos materials or they are damaged during the task
- EM2 - Training
- EM5 - Wetting asbestos materials
- EM6 - Personal protective equipment
- EM7 - Using rags to clean surfaces and equipment contaminated with asbestos
- EM8 - Personal decontamination

A16

TASK GUIDANCE SHEET

REMEMBER TO READ THE SAFETY CHECKLIST

ASBESTOS TASKS

Removal of asbestos paper linings

Equipment

- 500 gauge polythene sheeting and duct tape.

- Warning tape and notices.

- Sealant, select one low in hazardous constituents eg solvents.

- Scissors or knife.

- Bucket of water, garden type spray and rags.

- Suitable asbestos waste container, eg a labelled polythene sack.

- Appropriate llighting.

Description

This task guidance sheet can be used where asbestos paper linings need to be removed eg from a boiler casing. (Figure 47).

Only carry out this work if you are properly trained. See EM2 - Training.

Figure 47 Asbestos paper lining

Personal protective equipment (PPE)

- Disposable overalls fitted with a hood.

- Boots without laces (laced boots can be difficult to decontaminate).

- Disposable particulate respirator (FF P3).

Preparing the work area

- Carry out the work with the minimum number of people present.

- Restrict access, eg close the door and/or use warning tape and notices.

- Use polythene sheeting, secured with duct tape, to cover surfaces within the segregated area which could become contaminated.

- Ensure adequate lighting.

Removal

- Where necessary, make sure the system is electrically isolated.

- Carefully dismantle any casing around the paper lining, eg the metal covers on a boiler.

- Protect any vulnerable components with polythene sheeting.

- Dampen exposed paper.

REMEMBER TO READ THE SAFETY CHECKLIST

- If possible remove whole, alternatively, remove paper lining without tearing eg by cutting - dampen as you remove (Figure 48).

- Seal any paper which can't be removed.

Cleaning

- Use wet rags to clean the equipment.

- Use wet rags to clean the segregated area.

- Place debris, used rags, polythene sheeting and other waste in the waste container.

Figure 48 Removing asbestos paper lining from a section of boiler casing

Personal decontamination

- Use EM8 - Personal decontamination.

Clearance procedure

- Visually inspect the area to make sure that it has been properly cleaned.

- Clearance air sampling is not normally required.

What you need to read

- EM1 - What to do if you uncover asbestos materials or they are damaged during the task
- EM2 - Training
- EM5 - Wetting asbestos materials
- EM6 - Personal protective equipment
- EM7 - Using rags to clean surfaces and equipment contaminated with asbestos
- EM8 - Personal decontamination

A17

TASK GUIDANCE SHEET

REMEMBER TO READ THE SAFETY CHECKLIST

ASBESTOS TASKS

Removal of asbestos friction linings

Equipment

- 500 gauge polythene sheeting and duct tape.

- Warning tape and notices.

- Bucket of water, garden type spray and rags.

- Suitable asbestos waste container, eg a labelled polythene sack.

- Appropriate lighting.

Description

This task guidance sheet can be used where a friction lining, containing asbestos eg brake assemblies, clutch housings, needs to be removed from its housing or the housing needs to be cleaned (Figure 49).

Only carry out this work if you are properly trained. See EM2 - Training.

Figure 49 Brake lining

Personal protective equipment (PPE)

- Disposable overalls fitted with a hood.

- Boots without laces (laced boots can be difficult to decontaminate).

- Disposable particulate respirator (FF P3).

Preparing the work area

- Carry out the work with the minimum number of people present.

- Use warning tape and notices to restrict access.

- Use polythene sheeting, secured with duct tape, to cover any surface within the segregated area which could become contaminated, eg the floor beneath the housing.

- Ensure adequate lighting.

Removal

- Partially open the housing and spray the inside with water.

- Open housing.

- Use wet rags to clean inside the housing (Figure 50).

Figure 50 Cleaning housing

- Place worn friction lining and dirty rags in the waste container.

- If necessary, replace lining with a non-asbestos material.

Cleaning

- Use wet rags to clean the equipment.

- Use wet rags to wipe clean segregated area.

- Place debris, used rags, polythene sheeting and other waste in the waste container.

Personal decontamination

- Use EM8 - Personal decontamination.

Clearance procedure

- Visually inspect the area to make sure that it has been properly cleaned.

- Clearance air sampling is not normally required.

What you need to read

- EM1 - What to do if you uncover asbestos materials or they are damaged during the task
- EM2 - Training
- EM5 - Wetting asbestos materials
- EM6 - Personal protective equipment
- EM7 - Using rags to clean surfaces and equipment contaminated with asbestos
- EM8 - Personal decontamination

A18
TASK GUIDANCE SHEET

ASBESTOS TASKS

A19
TASK GUIDANCE SHEET

Removal of asbestos fire blankets

Equipment

■ Garden type spray and rags.

■ Suitable asbestos waste container, eg a labelled polythene sack.

■ Appropriate lighting.

Description

This task guidance sheet can be used where asbestos fire blankets need to be removed or replaced with suitable non-asbestos replacements (Figure 51).

Only carry out this work if you are properly trained. See EM2 - Training.

Figure 51 Fire blanket

Personal protective equipment (PPE)

■ Disposable overalls fitted with a hood.

■ Boots without laces (laced boots can be difficult to decontaminate).

■ A disposable particulate respirator (FF P3).

Preparing the work area

■ Carry out the work with the minimum number of people present.

■ Ensure adequate lighting.

Removal

■ Where the fire blanket and container are no longer required, unscrew the box from the wall and place in the waste container.

■ For blankets in boxes with opening bases, open the front to allow the blanket to fall into the waste container (Figure 52).

■ Where the blanket has to be pulled out of the base of a circular container, spray up into the container (pulling the blanket out dry can cause it to rub on the side of the container).

Figure 52 Fire blanket being removed (the sleeve of the overalls rolled up to aid clarity)

- Do not over wet as this will create a pool of water.

- Carefully pull the blanket out and place in the waste container.

- Do not unravel or shake the blanket.

Cleaning

- Use wet rags to clean inside the container.

Personal decontamination

- Use EM8 - Personal decontamination.

Clearance procedure

- Visually inspect the inside of the container and the floor etc, to make sure that it has been properly cleaned.

- Clearance air sampling is not normally required.

What you need to read

- EM1 - What to do if you uncover asbestos materials or they are damaged during the task
- EM2 - Training
- EM5 - Wetting asbestos materials
- EM6 - Personal protective equipment
- EM7 - Using rags to clean surfaces and equipment contaminated with asbestos
- EM8 - Personal decontamination

A19

TASK GUIDANCE SHEET

REMEMBER TO READ THE SAFETY CHECKLIST

ASBESTOS TASKS

A20
TASK GUIDANCE SHEET

Laying cables in areas containing undamaged asbestos materials

Equipment

- 500 gauge polythene sheeting and duct tape.

- Spray adhesive – select one low in hazardous constituents eg solvents.

- Warning tape and notices.

- Bucket of water and rags.

- Suitable asbestos waste container, eg a labelled polythene sack.

- Appropriate lighting.

Description

This task guidance sheet can be used where it may be necessary to run cables through an area containing undamaged asbestos lagging, coating or insulating board.

It is not appropriate where there is damaged asbestos material present.

Only carry out this work if you are properly trained. See EM2 - Training.

Personal protective equipment (PPE)

- Disposable overalls fitted with a hood.

- Boots without laces (laced boots can be difficult to decontaminate).

- Disposable particulate respirator (FF P3).

Preparing the work area

This work may be carried out at height, if so, the appropriate precautions to prevent the risk of falls MUST be taken.

- Use Task Guidance Sheet A2 - Removal of a single asbestos insulating board ceiling tile, if an asbestos ceiling tile needs to be removed to allow access.

- Carry out the work with the minimum number of people present.

- Restrict access, eg close the door and/or use warning tape and notices.

- Ensure adequate lighting.

Cable laying

- Do not run cables near asbestos lagging, coatings or insulating board.

- Where possible use existing cable trays or conduits or fix cables to non-asbestos surfaces (Figure 53). Do not fix through asbestos coatings.

REMEMBER TO READ THE SAFETY CHECKLIST

64

- Do not run cables over asbestos insulating board or lagging.

- If this is unavoidable, first protect the surface with duct tape or polythene sheeting secured with duct tape.

- Make sure cabling runs over the protected sections.

- Use duct tape and spray adhesive to tape the cable down to nearby non-asbestos surface.

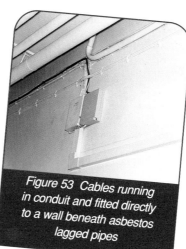

Figure 53 Cables running in conduit and fitted directly to a wall beneath asbestos lagged pipes

Cleaning

- Use wet rags to clean the equipment.

- Place debris, used rags, polythene sheeting and other waste in the waste container.

Personal decontamination

- Use EM8 - Personal decontamination.

Clearance procedure

- Visually inspect the area to make sure that it has been properly cleaned.

- Clearance air sampling is not normally required.

What you need to read

- *Tower scaffolds* Construction Information Sheet CIS10 HSE Books 1997
- *General access scaffolds and ladders* Construction Information Sheet CIS49 HSE Books 1997
- EM1 - What to do if you uncover asbestos materials or they are damaged during the task
- EM2 - Training
- EM6 - Personal protective equipment
- EM7 - Using rags to clean surfaces and equipment contaminated with asbestos
- EM8 - Personal decontamination

A20

TASK GUIDANCE SHEET

REMEMBER TO READ THE SAFETY CHECKLIST

ASBESTOS TASKS

Removal of asbestos-containing bituminous products

Equipment

- 500 gauge polythene sheeting and duct tape.

- Warning tape and notices.

- Sharp knife and scraper.

- Shovel.

- Bucket of water and rags.

- Suitable asbestos waste container eg a labelled polythene sack.

- Enclosed rubble chutes for roofwork - a series of interlocking plastic 'buckets' which run from the work area down to a lockable skip.

Description

This task guidance sheet can be used for the removal of asbestos-containing bituminous products, eg built-up roofing, gutter linings, damp proof course etc (Figure 54).

It is not appropriate for work with metal cladding lined with asbestos-containing bitumen (eg 'Galbestos') - use A22 - Removal of metal cladding lined with asbestos-containing bitumen.

Only carry out this work if you are properly trained. See EM2 - Training.

Figure 54 Built up bituminous roofing

Personal protective equipment (PPE)

- Disposable overalls fitted with a hood.

- Waterproof clothing may be required outside.

- Boots without laces (laced boots can be difficult to decontaminate).

- Disposable particulate respirator (FF P3).

Preparing the work area

This work may be carried out at height, if so, the appropriate precautions to prevent a risk of falls MUST be taken.

- Carry out the work with the minimum number of people present.

- Restrict access, eg use warning tape and notices.

- Use polythene sheeting and duct tape to seal any access points into the building eg skylights.

- It is dangerous to seal over exhaust vents from heating units in use.

REMEMBER TO READ THE SAFETY CHECKLIST

66

Removal

■ Consider overlaying with non-asbestos bituminous felt - note the presence of the covered asbestos material, or cut around the area to be removed. Avoid ripping (Figure 55).

Figure 55 Felt being cut and rolled up

■ To handle safely, remove manageable sections (for roofwork, place in the rubble chute) and place in the skip.

■ Remove any adhered material by dampening and gentle scraping.

■ Pick up debris.

■ Remove large deposits of dust by dampening and then shovelling into the waste container.

■ Dust and debris from disintegrating felt should be dampened and placed in the waste container.

■ Do not burn debris.

Cleaning

■ Use wet rags to clean the equipment.

■ Remove debris from segregated area.

■ Place debris, polythene sheeting, used rags and other waste in the waste container.

Personal decontamination

■ Use EM8 - Personal decontamination.

Clearance procedure

■ Visually inspect the area to make sure that it has been properly cleaned.

■ Clearance air sampling is not normally required.

What you need to read

■ *Health and safety in roof work* HSG33 HSE Books 1998 ISBN 0 7176 1425 5
■ *Tower scaffolds* Construction Information Sheet CIS10 HSE Books 1997
■ *General access scaffolds and ladders* Construction Information Sheet CIS49 HSE Books 1997
■ EM1 - What to do if you uncover asbestos materials or they are damaged during the task
■ EM2 - Training
■ EM5 - Wetting asbestos materials
■ EM6 - Personal protective equipment
■ EM7 - Using rags to clean surfaces and equipment contaminated with asbestos
■ EM8 - Personal decontamination

A21

TASK GUIDANCE SHEET

REMEMBER TO READ THE SAFETY CHECKLIST

A22
TASK GUIDANCE SHEET

Removal of metal cladding lined with asbestos-containing bitumen

Equipment

- 500 and 1000 gauge polythene sheeting and duct tape.

- Warning tape and notices.

- Bolt cutters.

- Hammer and chisel.

- Bucket of water, garden type spray and rags.

- Suitable asbestos waste container, eg a labelled polythene sack.

- Lockable skip - for larger quantities of metal cladding.

- Asbestos warning stickers.

- Appropriate lighting.

Description

This task guidance sheet can be used for the removal of metal cladding lined with asbestos-containing bitumen (eg 'Galbestos').

It is not appropriate for work with asbestos-containing bitumen such as roofing felt and damp proof courses - use A21 - Removal of asbestos-containing bituminous products.

Only carry out this work if you are properly trained. See EM2 - Training.

Personal protective equipment (PPE)

- Disposable overalls fitted with a hood.

- Waterproof clothing may be required outside.

- Boots without laces (laced boots can be difficult to decontaminate).

- Disposable particulate respirator (FF P3).

Preparing the work area

This work may be carried out at height, if so, the appropriate precautions to prevent the risk of falls MUST be taken.

- Carry out the work with the minimum number of people present.

- Restrict access eg close the door and/or use warning tape and notices.

- Use 500 gauge polythene sheeting, secured with duct tape, to cover any surface within the segregated area which could become contaminated.

- It is dangerous to seal over exhaust vents from heating units in use.

- Ensure adequate lighting.

Removal

- Carefully remove any fixtures attached to the cladding, eg pipework.

- If the sheets are screwed in place, use a hammer and chisel to knock off the screw heads.

- If the sheets are bolted in place, cut using bolt cutters avoiding contact with the asbestos-containing bitumen (Figure 56).

- Pull the sheet away from the fastenings.

- Lower to the ground - do not use rubble chutes.

- Check for debris in screw or bolt holes. Clean with wet rags.

- Place small items and debris in the waste container.

- Small pieces of metal cladding can be double wrapped in 1000 gauge polythene sheeting (or placed in waste containers if small enough). Attach asbestos warning stickers.

- Where there are several sheets of metal cladding, place in a lockable skip.

Figure 56 Screw attachment on a damaged Galbestos sheet

Cleaning

- Use wet rags to clean the equipment.

- Use wet rags to clean the segregated area.

- Place debris and used rags and other waste in the waste container.

Personal decontamination

- Use EM8 - Personal decontamination.

Clearance procedure

- Visually inspect the area to make sure that it has been properly cleaned.

- Clearance air sampling is not normally required.

What you need to read

- *Health and safety in roof work* HSG33 HSE Books 1998 ISBN 0 7176 1425 5
- *Tower scaffolds* Construction Information Sheet CIS10 HSE Books 1997
- *General access scaffolds and ladders* Construction Information Sheet CIS49 HSE Books 1997
- EM1 - What to do if you uncover asbestos materials or they are damaged during the task
- EM2 - Training
- EM5 - Wetting asbestos materials
- EM6 - Personal protective equipment
- EM7 - Using rags to clean surfaces and equipment contaminated with asbestos
- EM8 - Personal decontamination

A22

TASK GUIDANCE SHEET

REMEMBER TO READ THE SAFETY CHECKLIST

A23
TASK GUIDANCE SHEET

Removal of asbestos-containing floor tiles

Equipment

- Warning tape and notices.

- Type H vacuum cleaner to BS5415 for large areas

- Scraper, shovel, hammer and knife.

- Bucket of water, garden type spray and rags.

- Suitable asbestos waste container, eg a labelled polythene sack.

- Appropriate lighting.

Description

This task guidance sheet can be used for the removal of asbestos-containing floor tiles (Figure 57).

Only carry out this work if you are properly trained. See EM2 - Training.

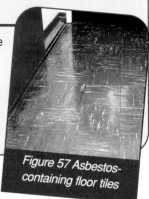

Figure 57 Asbestos-containing floor tiles

Personal protective equipment (PPE)

- Disposable overalls fitted with a hood.

- Boots without laces (laced boots can be difficult to decontaminate).

- Disposable particulate respirator (FF P3).

Preparing the work area

- Carry out the work with the minimum number of people present.

- Restrict access, eg close the door and/or use warning tape and notices.

- Ensure adequate lighting.

Removal

- Consider overlaying the floor with a non-asbestos material

- Note the presence of the asbestos floor tiles so that it can be managed.

- Alternatively, place scraper in joint between tiles and gently lift, minimising breakage (Figure 58).

Figure 58 Tiles being removed

- Where there are a large number of tiles to remove use a shovel. This speeds up the job and prevents you kneeling close to the tiles.

REMEMBER TO READ THE SAFETY CHECKLIST

- Use the hammer to tap the scraper between the joints of firmly adhered tiles.

- Spray water under the tiles as they are lifted as asbestos paper may be present.

- Wet any asbestos paper backing as the tiles are lifted.

- Gently scrape up adhered mastic - this can be heated to aid removal.

- Do not sand floor.

- Place debris in the waste container.

Cleaning

- A Type H vacuum cleaner can be used to clean large floor areas.

- Where only a few tiles have been removed use wet rags to clean the floor.

- Use wet rags to clean the equipment.

- Remove visible debris from segregated area and place, along with used rags and other waste in the waste container.

Personal decontamination

- Use EM8 - Personal decontamination.

Clearance procedure

- Visually inspect the area to make sure that it has been properly cleaned.

- Clearance air sampling is not normally required.

What you need to read

- EM1 - What to do if you uncover asbestos materials or they are damaged during the task
- EM2 - Training
- EM4 - Using a Type H vacuum cleaner when working with asbestos
- EM5 - Wetting asbestos materials
- EM6 - Personal protective equipment
- EM7 - Using rags to clean surfaces and equipment contaminated with asbestos
- EM8 - Personal decontamination

A23

TASK GUIDANCE SHEET

REMEMBER TO READ THE SAFETY CHECKLIST

ASBESTOS TASKS

Removal of flexible asbestos textile duct connectors

Equipment

- Warning tape and notices.

- Drill.

- Screwdriver.

- Metal scraper.

- Bucket of water, garden type spray and rags.

- Suitable asbestos waste container, eg a labelled polythene sack.

- Appropriate lighting.

Figure 59 Rivetted connector

Description

This task guidance sheet can be used where a flexible asbestos textile connector (gaiter) needs to be removed from between sections of metal ductwork or the joint with a fan. It can be used where the flexible connector is riveted to the metal frame or where it is placed over the ducting and clipped in place. Two methods are given:

Method 1 - Removal of riveted duct connectors (Figure 59).
Method 2 - Removal of duct connectors placed over the duct and clipped in place (Figure 60).

Only carry out this work if you are properly trained. See EM2 - Training.

Personal protective equipment (PPE)

- Disposable overalls fitted with a hood.

- Boots without laces (laced can be difficult to decontaminate).

- Disposable particulate respirator (FF P3).

Preparation of work area

This work may be carried out at height, if so, the appropriate precautions to prevent a risk of falls MUST be taken.

- Sections of riveted connectors may be heavy - handle with care.

- Carry out the work with the minimum number of people present.

- Restrict access, eg close door and/ or use warning tape and notices.

- Ensure adequate lighting.

Removal - general

- Before starting work check that the adjacent ducting is not lagged with asbestos.

- If it is you will need to employ a specialist contractor licensed by HSE if the material could be disturbed.

- Turn off and lock the system.

REMEMBER TO READ THE SAFETY CHECKLIST

Method 1

- Where possible, unbolt the assembly holding the connector and remove whole.

- Remove or dampen the connector and drill out the rivets, avoiding the flexible connector.

- Ease the metal plate away and dampen the connector.

- Remove from the metal plate.

- Dampen any adhered material and carefully scrape into the waste container.

Figure 60 Clipped connector

Method 2

- Dampen the flexible connector.

- Remove the clip holding the connector in place.

- Slide connector off the ducting and place in a waste container.

- Dampen any debris adhering to screw holes or ducting.

- Carefully scrape into the waste container.

Cleaning

- Use wet rags to clean the equipment.

- Use wet rags to clean the segregated area.

- Place debris, used rags and other waste in the waste container.

Personal decontamination

- Use EM8 - Personal decontamination.

Clearance procedure

- Visually inspect the area to make sure that it has been properly cleaned.

- Clearance air sampling is not normally required.

What you need to read

- *Tower scaffolds Construction* Information Sheet CIS10 HSE Books 1997
- *General access scaffolds and ladders* Construction Information Sheet CIS49 HSE Books 1997
- EM1 - What to do if you uncover asbestos materials or they are damaged during the task
- EM2 - Training
- EM5 - Wetting asbestos materials
- EM6 - Personal protective equipment
- EM7 - Using rags to clean surfaces and equipment contaminated with asbestos
- EM8 - Personal decontamination

A24

TASK GUIDANCE SHEET

REMEMBER TO READ THE SAFETY CHECKLIST

A25
TASK GUIDANCE SHEET

Removal of compressed asbestos fibre gaskets and asbestos rope seals

Equipment

- 500 gauge polythene sheeting and duct tape.

- Warning tape and notices.

- Type H vacuum cleaner to BS5415 - needed where residual gasket material may be adhered to one or more surfaces (Figure 62).

- Metal scraper.

- Bucket of water, garden type spray and rags.

- Suitable asbestos waste container, eg a labelled polythene sack.

- Appropriate lighting.

Description

This task guidance sheet can be used for the removal of compressed asbestos fibre gaskets and asbestos rope seals from pipework, vessels, plant or other equipment such as domestic heaters and boilers (Figure 61).

Only carry out this work if you are properly trained. See EM2 – Training.

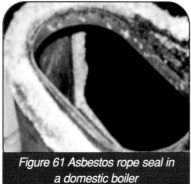

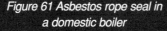

Figure 61 Asbestos rope seal in a domestic boiler

Figure 62 Gasket material adhering to a pipe flange

Personal protective equipment (PPE)

- Disposable overalls fitted with a hood.

- Boots without laces (laced boots can be difficult to decontaminate).

- Disposable particulate respirator (FF P3).

Preparing the work area

This work may be carried out at height, if so, the appropriate precautions to prevent the risk of falls MUST be taken.

- Carry out the work with the minimum number of people present.

- Restrict access - eg close the door and/or use warning tape and notices.

- Use polythene sheeting, secured with duct tape, to cover surfaces within the segregated area which could become contaminated.

- Ensure adequate lighting.

REMEMBER TO READ THE SAFETY CHECKLIST

Removal

- Ensure that the system is switched off or has been made safe, eg pipework emptied of its contents, electrical supply isolated etc.

- Unbolt/unscrew the flange or dismantle the equipment.

- Protect any vulnerable components with polythene sheeting.

- Once the gasket/rope seal is accessible, dampen (Figure 63).

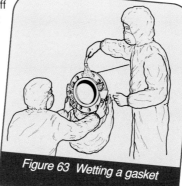

Figure 63 Wetting a gasket

- Further expose the gasket and continue dampening.

- Use the scraper to ease the gasket/rope seal away.

- Place in the waste container.

- Check surfaces for residual gasket/rope seal (Figure 61).

- Keeping it damp, gently scrape away the residual gasket/rope.

- If there is a lot of residual material, gently scrape away using shadow vacuuming.

Cleaning

- Use wet rags to wipe clean the equipment.

- Use wet rags and the Type H vacuum cleaner if available to clean the segregated area.

- Place used rags, polythene sheeting and other waste in the waste containers.

Personal decontamination

- Use EM8 - Personal decontamination.

Clearance procedure

- Visually inspect the area to make sure that it has been properly cleaned.

- Clearance air sampling is not normally required.

What you need to read

- *Safety of electrical motor-operated industrial and commercial cleaning appliances. Particular requirements. Specification for vacuum cleaners, wet and/or dry* BS 5415 2.2 Supplement No 1: 1986
- *Tower scaffolds* Construction Information Sheet CIS10 HSE Books 1997
- *General access scaffolds and ladders* Construction Information Sheet CIS49 HSE Books 1997
- EM1 - What to do if you uncover asbestos materials or they are damaged during the task
- EM2 - Training
- EM4 - Using a Type H vacuum cleaner when working with asbestos
- EM5 - Wetting asbestos materials
- EM6 - Personal protective equipment
- EM7 - Using rags to clean surfaces and equipment contaminated with asbestos
- EM8 - Personal decontamination

A25

TASK GUIDANCE SHEET

REMEMBER TO READ THE SAFETY CHECKLIST

Printed and published by the Health and Safety Executive   04/01   C150